EXCEPT THE COLOR GREY

ARLENE ALDA

TUNDRA BOOKS

Published in Canada by Tundra Books,
75 Sherbourne Street, Toronto, Ontario M5A 2P9

Published in the United States by Tundra Books of Northern New York,
P.O. Box 1030, Plattsburgh, New York 12901

Library of Congress Control Number: 2011920223

Library and Archives Canada Cataloguing in Publication

Alda, Arlene, 1933-
    Except the color grey / Arlene Alda.

ISBN 978-1-77049-284-4

    1. Colors–Juvenile literature. 2. Senses and sensation– Juvenile literature. I. Title.

QC495.5.A43 2011   j535.6   C2011-900451-8

We acknowledge the financial support of the Government of Canada through the Book Publishing Industry Development Program (BPIDP) and that of the Government of Ontario through the Ontario Media Development Corporation's Ontario Book Initiative. We further acknowledge the support of the Canada Council for the Arts and the Ontario Arts Council for our publishing program.

ONTARIO ARTS COUNCIL
CONSEIL DES ARTS DE L'ONTARIO

Design: Leah Springate

Printed and bound in China

1 2 3 4 5 6   16 15 14 13 12 11

For Alan

Which **color** is my favorite?

But RED is just the opposite.

It's very hard to say. I like most colors that I see,

Except the color GREY.

GREY is clouds without the sun.
GREY is dreary dark.

Do I like BLUE? I do, I do!
I ride BLUE to the beach.

BLUE is there while hugging friends;
too many, though, to reach.

YELLOW's awesome on a face.

It's tempting on the street.

Then there's ORANGE, bold and bright –

On fruit: a juicy treat.

GREEN is great, I must admit.
It's soft, just like a bed.

It also makes me laugh out loud,
when piled on William's head.

The color PURPLE? On my list.

These grape balloons are why.

BLACK, BROWN, WHITE,

Or RUSTY brown. Hard to pass them by.

So many colors filled my eyes while I was out today.

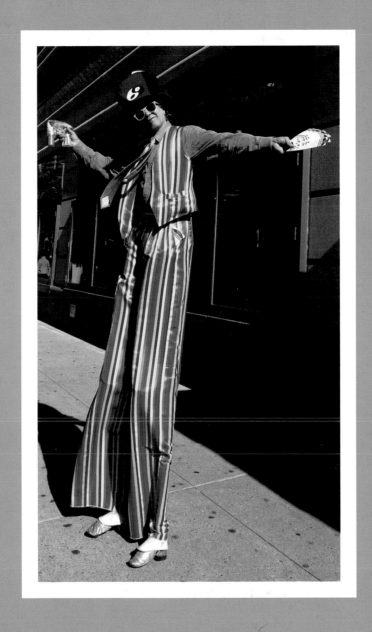

My favorite one? I've made up my mind.

It's home on my bunny.

It's GREY!!!

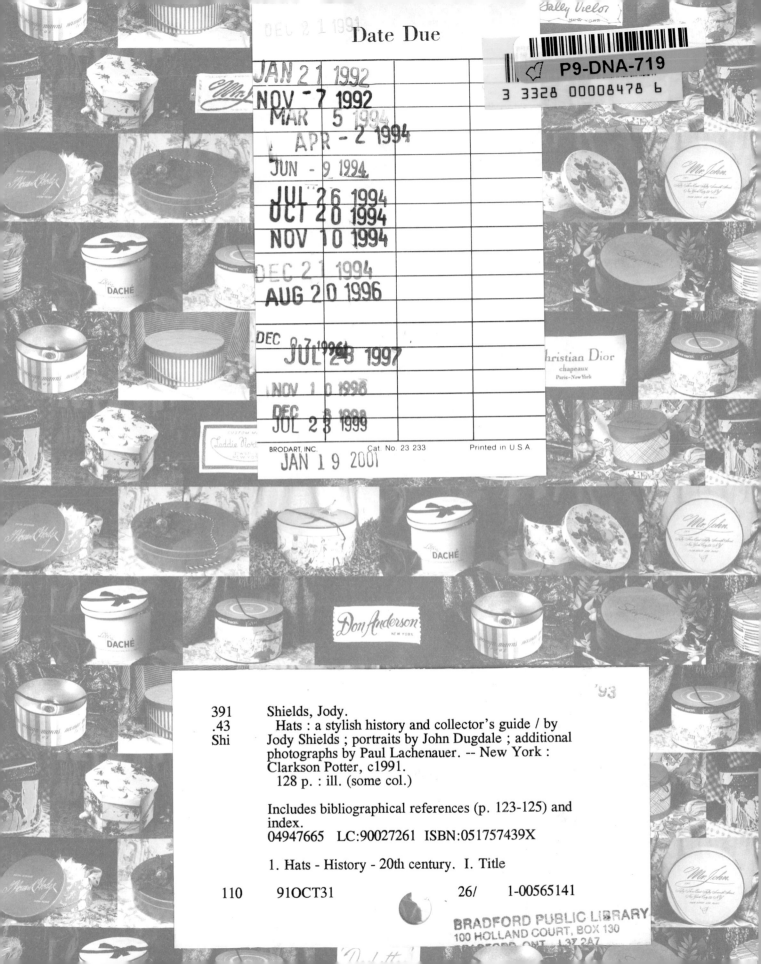

hats

hats

a stylish history and collector's guide

[by jody shields]

portraits by john dugdale

additional photographs
by paul lachenauer

design by helene silverman

Clarkson Potter/Publishers
New York

T O

Bernard F. Lennon

and

Gary Rubinstein

Published by Clarkson N. Potter, Inc.,
201 East 50th Street, New York, New
York 10022. Member of the Crown
Publishing Group.
CLARKSON N. POTTER, POTTER
and colophon are trademarks of
Clarkson N. Potter, Inc.
Manufactured in Japan

Library of Congress
Cataloging-in-Publication Data
Shields, Jody.
   Hats: a stylish history and
collector's guide/Jody Shields;
portraits by John Dugdale.
   p.   cm.
   ISBN 0-517-57439-X
   1. Hats—History—20th
century.   I. Title.
GT2110.S52 1991   90-27261
391'.43—dc20   CIP
10 9 8 7 6 5 4 3 2 1
First Edition

PAGE 1: feather chapeau, 1950s; **PAGE** 2; velvet hat, 1930s; **PAGE** 3: two hats by Don Marshall, 1950s; **PAGE** 5: felt beanie, late 1930s (brooch added); **PAGE** 6: capot, 1964.

CONTE

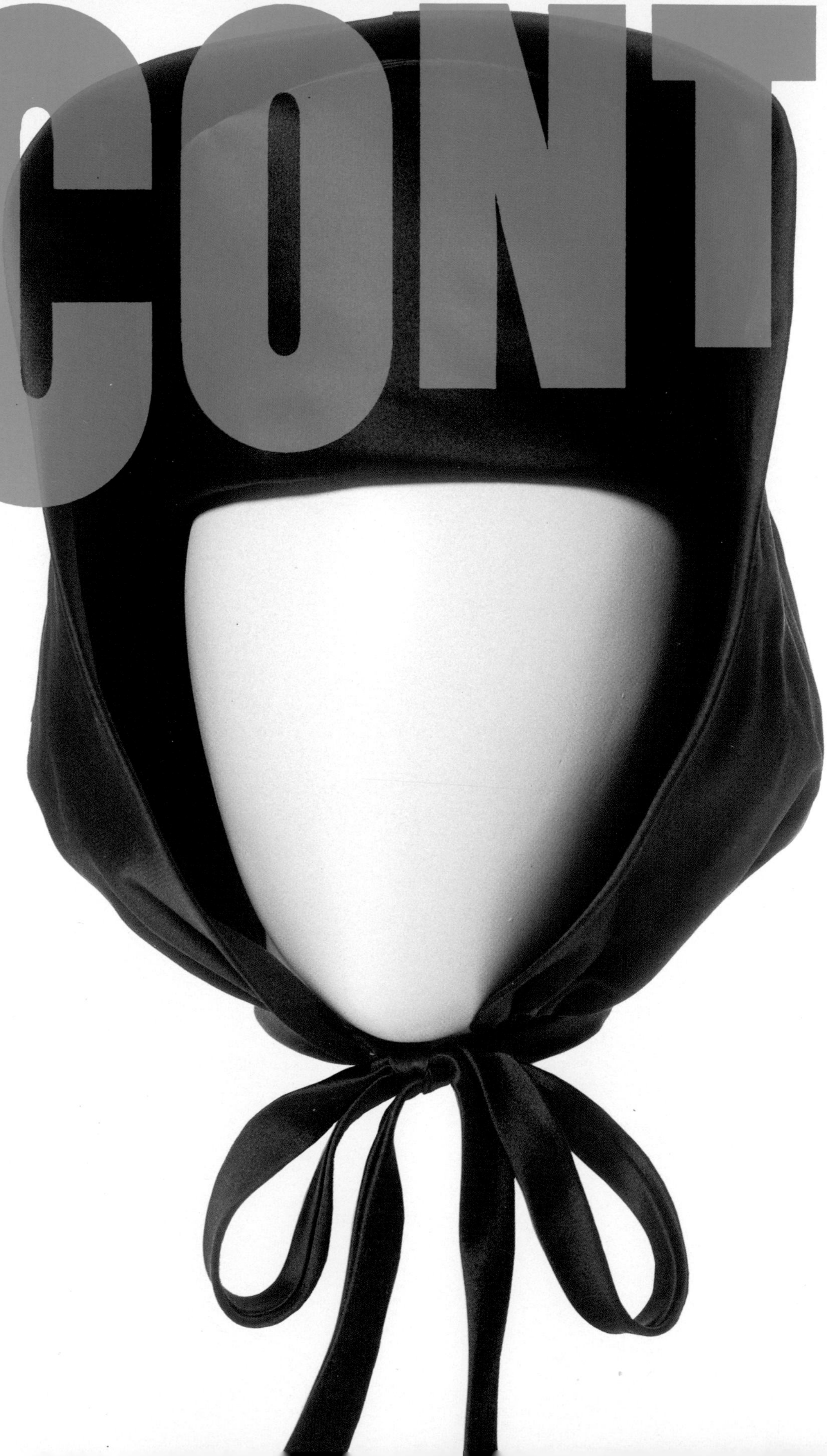

NTS

Millinery—and all

the customs that accompanied it—tops fashion's extinct list. The hat-fitting ritual has vanished. So has the knack of positioning the hat on the head correctly. Maneuvering the veil aside for cigarettes or an application of lipstick is a lost art. The fine-tuned understanding of the correct hat for each hour and season has nearly passed from living memory. Also lost is a therapeutic pleasure documented by *Harper's Bazaar* in 1930: the "if-you-are-discouraged-go-buy-a-hat philosophy."

A pair of spectator sports have also fallen from practice. They are the view-obstructing hat, which plagued theaters, and the practice of eyeballing headgear. The truly chic could decipher a woman's status by a single glance at her hat. As *Fashionable Dress* magazine reported in

[introduction]

"Chic requires nothing at all. It is much more the way you carry your head than the way you wear your clothes." —PRINCESS LUCIEN MURAT

9

1925, that code-breaking activity dominated lunch at the Ritz in Paris: "The best of the new hats, if one prolongs one's luncheon awhile, will eventually make an appearance. Enfin, it reaches a point whether the real object of one's visit is the quest of food or chapeaux. He must be a clever chef who competes with milliners Reboux and Lewis these days." This fierce peer-group patrolling kept women locked into the cult of millinery for at least half the 20th century.

In the 1920s the millinery cult was also fueled by a new development, coordinated accessories—matching hats, bags, belts, gloves, and shoes—which confirmed the hat's importance. In the 1920s and early 1930s, a handful of Parisian milliners became fashion powerhouses; certain millinery labels carried the same weight as those of the great couturiers. However, as couturiers expanded the scope of their empire to include accessories—another way to stamp their look on their clients—their hats gradually eclipsed the work of the milli-

The 1950s hat by Don Marshall, **PAGE 8**, shows the height of the "coordinated look." Neither the techniques of hat construction—nor the working scene—have changed since the 1950s scene in a Paris atelier was taken, **BELOW**. Graphic labels, like the one from Sally Victor, **OPPOSITE**, who started her company in 1934, mark fashion's finest hats.

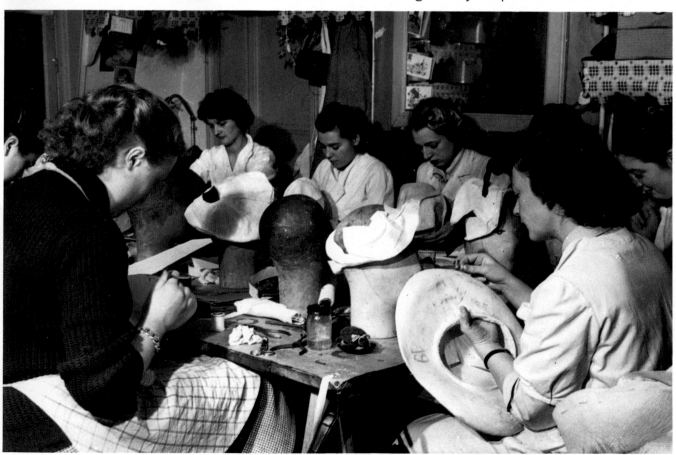

nery specialists, launching the real Golden Age of fashionable hats.

During this period, a fashion item with a Paris label (or a Paris-inspired copy of it) was the first and last word. Every single season, the collections presented in Paris were studied and obeyed. Millinery was a sensitive barometer of style changes, created to accommodate

the cut of collars and décolletté, the width of shoulders, length of earrings and hemlines, and even the size, shape, and frequency of buttons. Accordingly, every season, hat brims shrank or expanded, crowns telescoped up or down, trimmings blossomed or were pruned back.

In the 1930s, American millinery began to acquire its own cachet, although styles were still dictated by Paris. It was a common practice for American millinery manufacturers to purchase original hats and garments in Paris and ship them by the fastest ocean liner to New York, where they were copied line for line. There was no shame in advertising a hat as a "copy of an Agnès original." Top stores offered these reproductions side by side with the more expensive originals that inspired them. The challenge for the fashionable woman was to flaunt her fresh-from-Paris chapeau before the copies hit town.

The society woman of New York and Paris had an influence just as powerful as that of the couturiers. Her custom-made millinery, spotted at the right restaurant or the theater, could set a style seen 'round the world. Also influential were the international expositions and fairs, fashion's wild cards in the 1920s, 1930s, and 1940s. Millinery borrowed shamelessly from the native headgear of the exhibiting countries, including Morocco, Thailand, India, and South America.

In the 1940s, World War II changed the means and the mode of millinery. Ingenuity and handicraft filled the gap caused by a shortage

VOGUE

Pre-Spring Hats
New prints
New pick-ups

Incorporating Vanity Fair January 15.1945 Price 35 Cents 40 Cents In Canada

of materials and fashion input from Paris. Although the handmade hat had a slightly crude and ad-libbed quality, it also boasted a certain peculiar charm—and it was the patriotic thing to do. Even professionally produced hats appeared as if they had been made at home by rather clumsy loving hands.

Millinery managed to survive these difficulties, but a pair of new developments KO'd the chapeau in the 1950s. Hats couldn't fight the increasingly ornate hairdos and an increasingly casual lifestyle. The hairdo became the hat's arch rival with the introduction of hairspray. From 1954 to 1957, hairspray sales leaped 280 percent while hat sales slumped 31 percent. Once hairdressers built hair into high-rising, lacquered, bouffant sculptures, hats lost their foothold on the head. By decade's end, hats were reduced to a miserly fluff of veiling or a hair bow, and milliners created the wig toque—a hat that mimicked hair.

Ultimately deadlier than towering hair was the rise of casual dress, although there were holdouts in the de rigueur hat camp as late as the mid-1950s. Gossip columnist Hedda Hopper, famed for her mad hattery, was an example, along with the women of San Francisco. After the Republican convention in that city in 1956, Hopper tartly observed to the magazine *Hats* that "some of the visiting ladies had red faces because they brought no hats; they learned the hard way that in this city a woman would sooner go without her shoes as without a hat.'' But by then Hedda Hopper's opinion was hardly in the majority.

By the 1960s, the hat was resigned to its place as an anachronism, a quaint accessory. An international roster of hairdressers (Kenneth, Vidal Sassoon, Alexandre) replaced milliners as chief head decorators. Supplemented with wigs, falls, switches, and hairpieces—or cut into a simple geometrical shape—hair was in its glory. The attitude was summed up by film actress Brigitte Bardot, who pouted, ''I don't like hats. I prefer my hair. It is part of my personality, undisciplined like me.'' In the next decade, fashion was split between disco dressing and dressing for success, and neither option held a place for millinery.

When couturier Christian Lacroix's elaborate, fanciful fashions sailed into the 1980s, they towed the hat in their wake. With the revival of interest in a more dressed and accessorized style, hats made a comeback—not as an everyday item, but as a dramatic special-occasion accessory. A hat became the signature of the more radical, forward-thinking fashionables. A handful of contemporary milliners even acquired international reputations: Stephan Jones and Kristin Woodward of London, Philippe Model of Paris, and Manolo of New York.

This sign of the times would have been welcome news to couturier Christian Dior, who declared emphatically in 1957: ''I consider that without hats, an intrinsic part of fashion, we would have no civilization.''

The cover of *Vogue* was a prime showcase for millinery through the 1960s. The high-rising helmet, **BELOW**, complemented severe, shaped clothes in 1963. Equally dramatic, **OPPOSITE**, is a toque with a face-masking veil.

the 20s

"we moderns" triumph

Though thoroughly denounced in her day, the flapper did have endearing qualities: her jazz-baby, slang-studded vocabulary, fiercely cultivated bad manners, and insistence on the title "modern." Drooping posture—the "debutante slouch"—was her trademark. As author/photographer and social moth Cecil Beaton observed, these affected types were women who would "rather smoke than eat." It's no wonder that smoking was popular, since it drew attention to the

Women today have all the charm of a male impersonator.   —CECIL BEATON

mouth—practically the only part of a woman's face not covered by her cloche hat. It's also no wonder the flapper preferred cigarettes to food, since clothing left the neck, arms, legs, and back uncovered—all the better to display a figure that had ''a curveless similarity to a boa constrictor,'' as *Vogue* drily described it.

The flapper also had her precious

There was an appropriate garment —and accessories—for the time, place, and even hours of the day and night. To be well dressed required a delicate understanding of these minute details. To help their readers arrive at this perfect state, women's magazines exhaustively charted hour-by-hour proper attire. For instance, a truly fashionable woman would never go out

in shoes with Cuban heels in the evening, wear an exotic flower corsage in the morning, or put on a straw hat before May. Beginning around 1923 and continuing for the rest of the decade, women followed a daily millinery schedule of small, severe, and chic headgear in the morning; larger-brimmed, more feminine hats for formal afternoon events; and elaborately

contradictions: white fur-trimmed coats for summer, jewelry of real wood, fake diamonds, and flimsy, simple dresses decorated with elaborate beading. While she had the freedom to ''practically live in bathing suits and coconut oil,'' as *Vogue* noted, she was also compelled to change into proper dress for three o'clock tea.

The classic cloche dominated the decade, **PAGE 14**, but wide-brimmed hats flourished simultaneously. Styles ranged from the stitched straw hat with a turned-up brim (label: Tappe), **ABOVE**, to the panorama of hats created for sunning at the beach, **OPPOSITE**.

decorated hats in the evening. Hats just for resort wear were another variable. Although sportswear revolutionized fashion, creating a more casual dress code, that casualness never crossed over into millinery: hatlessness was never an option. Instead, milliners invented a new type of headgear exclusively for sportswear.

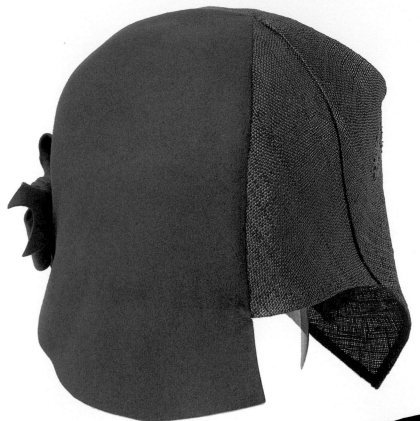

Suzanne Talbot, and Rose Valois. Jean Patou, Chanel, Paul Poiret, and Lucien Lelong were notable couturiers who also created hats. Their work was copied as soon as it could be pulled off the boat from France, and the imitations were advertised as "copies," along with the designer's name. For instance, a Saks Fifth Avenue ad of 1927 offered an original Marie-Alphonsine hat for $75, or "our exact copy, $18.75." At the other extreme, $155.52 could buy an entire noncouturier season wardrobe, as calculated by a magazine a few months later. Mail-order catalogues, local milliners, and home-sewn hats were other options for the fashion-conscious.

Despite the predominance of a handful of designers, millinery in the

Although women's magazines offered no real practical advice, such as which hats were most flattering for an individual's face shape, they devoted pages to correct dressing. One factor that did affect hat choice was taken for granted: a woman's age. There was a specific category of headwear for girls and the youthful flappers. Less-stylish to dull hats suited older married women and matrons.

One choice the magazines did make perfectly clear: an original from Paris was the most desirable hat. The great French couturiers and milliners were familiar names to American women who followed fashion magazines and newspaper store advertisements. A roll call of stellar hatters included Agnès, Rose Descat, Le Monnier, Marie-Alphonsine, Maria Guy, Reboux, J.

early 1920s was a mishmash that seemed to operate under the slogan "Anything goes." There was a bewildering assortment of styles, shapes, and sizes that stumped even fashion experts. "In fact, in millinery as in garments this year, the styles are almost chaotic in their variety, reflecting the general upset conditions in the world at large," sighed *Dry Goods Economist* in 1921. The lineup of chapeau influences for the year included monarchs (pharaohs, Charles II, and Napoleon), painters (Gainsborough and Watteau), adventurers (Captain Kidd, Breton sailors, and storybook cavaliers), and even Chinese pagodas. Neater silhouettes took the tennis goddess Suzanne Lenglen and the heavenly goddess Diana as models: heads were wrapped,

The chapeau silhouette waxed and waned as the decade progressed. Brimless styles included the unadorned model of finely woven straw (label: Northridge), **OPPOSITE ABOVE**, and the gold lace and silk cloche enriched with soutache, **ABOVE**. By 1927, the hat with a brim was de rigueur even for schoolgirls, as shown in the advertisement, **OPPOSITE BELOW**. A sports hat made up in wildly colored cotton print, **LEFT**, is an example of the "moderne" mode (label: Kilpin, Ltd., London).

bandeau fashion, with tinsel cloths.

Small hats perched like odd feathered nests, folded around the crown as stiffly as newspaper, or circled the head like a lumpy halo. Brims ranged from small to platter-sized, and flip-flopped up, down, and even sideways. Practically anything portable served as trimming: monstrous flowers; loop-the-loop swags of ribbon, drapery, and veiling; fruit, feathers (from chicken to vulture), leaves, and beads. Compared to the cumbersome hats of the early 'teens, these heavily decorated hats had a lightweight quality, since they were built on a delicate base of horsehair, stiffened lace, or woven straw.

While trimmings stayed constant, the scale of the hat was tuned to the dress silhouette and the rise and fall of hemlines. The narrow, close-fitting hat suited the short, simple dress; wider millinery balanced dresses broadened by umbrella gores, accordion pleats, inserts, godets, flying panels, drapery, and pouffs. "The extremely wide-brimmed hat with the knee-length gown—an absurdity. One laughs at the over-balanced figure," chuckled *Millinery Trade Review* in 1922.

The ultimate accessory—the automobile—also affected the balance of style. An English society magazine, *The Sketch,* claimed it was *le dernier cri* to harmonize the dress with the car. Lavishly garnished, super-scale leghorns and picture hats were obviously impractical for driving, even at the hardly breakneck top speed of 15 miles per hour. In 1920, hats made of leather—which could stand up to the velocity of car travel and the abuse of suitcase packing—were recommended for vacationing wardrobes. The switch to smaller, practical toppers didn't come easily. They were singled out by critics as "headgear of ugliness inconceivable," which represented what *Millinery Trade Review* called the "new and horrific era of dress."

The "horrific era" also ushered in technical innovations that gave cloth-

ing and millinery a new ease. Around 1918, the couturier Madeleine Vionnet removed the cumbersome lining and awkward buttons and hooks from dresses, so that the bias-cut garments simply slipped on, self-shaped to the wearer's body. Hats did likewise. By the summer of 1920, the Paris correspondent for *Millinery Trade Review* noted that hats also had fewer "bones" (buckram and stiffening), and often had only enough wire to slightly shape

the crown and brim. These unconstructed, flexible hats were lighter in weight and more comfortable than their predecessors, and permitted "the delightful custom of shaping the hat on the customer's head and seeing that her headwear became part of her individuality." The "popover" hat was an example of that new, flexible engineering. The popover resembled a collapsed chef's toque, with a high, puffy soft crown that rose to a mushroom shape, then flopped over the brim.

Once hats broke free of rigid construction, a new vocabulary of materials was introduced, with ribbon the perfect and flexible choice. Strips of half-inch- to 18-inch-wide taffeta, satin, grosgrain, and even lacquered and gilded snake, alligator, lizard, and carp skin were overlapped and stitched together into floppy hats. Braided straw, wool, and crepe fabrics were also supple enough for this type of construction. Ribbons were favored as trim, as well as basic material—double-faced, double-colored ribbons snaked into pompons and choux. Cut and curled, they resembled feathers. Bow-tied with trailing ends, ribbons goofily topped hats like airplane wings.

From 1924 until around 1926, a masculine style—called "garçonne" after Victor Marguerites' scandalous novel of the same name—directed fashion. This androgynous style included swagger topcoats and suits in rough tweeds, waistcoats, ascots, neckties, even decorative watch fobs, pocket handkerchiefs, and pince-nez. Couturier Lucien Lelong made the radical offering of culotte suits; Jean Patou and Chanel created two-piece menswear suits in wool jersey. "One affects girlishness by affecting boyishness," was *Fashionable Dress*'s shoulder-shrugging analysis.

The severely cropped garçonne haircut accompanied the refined garçonne look. The well-shaped head was essential to 1920s beauty, and it was mercilessly displayed by both the garçonne cut and the cloche. Cecil Beaton silkily expounded on the desired effect: "We flatten our hair on purpose to make it

sleek and silky and to show the shape of our skulls, and it is our supreme object to have a head looking like a wet football on a neck as thin as a governess's hat pin." *Fashionable Dress* made a prediction: "Just so long as that . . . insouciant coiffure known as the shingled bob remains in vogue, so long shall we have smaller hats."

The smaller hat—represented by the cloche—remained a standard until around 1927. Even though it was primarily a one-note style, each season brought an innovation: colors and textures changed; brims and trims appeared and disappeared; the face was concealed and revealed.

Fussy, ornate decoration coexisted with the standard streamlined style. The cloche, **OPPOSITE**, of 1925, features an enormous bow and ribbon decoration. Oak leaves smother the cloche (label: Henri Bendel), **ABOVE LEFT**; and, in an earlier example of excess, silk violets and orchids sprout from a lumpy-shaped toque, **BELOW LEFT**.

In 1925, the milliner Reboux introduced a helmetlike variation of the cloche, which reigned for the rest of the decade. The helmet was tight-fitting, narrow, and mushroomed into a high-peaked, round, and later a square crown, dented down the center like a fedora by manipulation (folded or dented by hand) or construction (a crown made with tucks, pleats, or in multiple sections). Sometimes topped with a colossal bow, which added even more height, helmets had tiny and irregular brims, usually snapped to the crown at front, sides, or back. Hem-

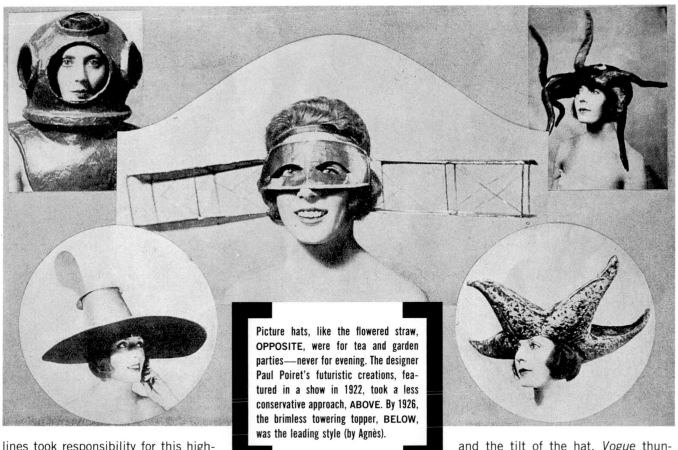

Picture hats, like the flowered straw, **OPPOSITE**, were for tea and garden parties—never for evening. The designer Paul Poiret's futuristic creations, featured in a show in 1922, took a less conservative approach, **ABOVE**. By 1926, the brimless towering topper, **BELOW**, was the leading style (by Agnès).

lines took responsibility for this high-rising hat. "The critics of fashion's inconsistencies are once more confounded. For as skirts became shorter, crowns appropriately became higher. What is lost at one end is gained at the other," quipped *Fashionable Dress*. The durable helmet topper crossed seasons and materials, fabricated in everything from straw to satin, although malleable felt was the favorite. Decorations ranged from sewn and draped details to simple bows to lashings of ostrich feathers.

A year after its introduction, the helmet's motto was "A maximum of crown and a minimum of brim." Varying their exaggerated upward zoom, hats projected out from the back of the head. Fashionable women fretted about the right brim, the right crown—

and the tilt of the hat. *Vogue* thundered that the high-crowned hat "becomes preposterous, even grotesque, when worn at any angle." Speaking *"ex cathedra," Vogue* urged women to keep their hats perfectly straight on their heads. As its silhouette became more outlandish, the hat lost much of its trimming—a bit of grosgrain, a single flower, feather, or bow were typical.

In 1927, an unlikely fashion influence made a debut: Charles Lindbergh. After his historic New York–Paris flight, "Lucky Lindy lids" appeared in his honor. Made of felt, the Lindy lid resembled a cloche, but had ear flaps similar to those of an aviator's helmet or the propellers of an airplane. Priced from $5 to $10, the lids even featured theme decorations, including tiny jeweled airplanes, wings and pro-

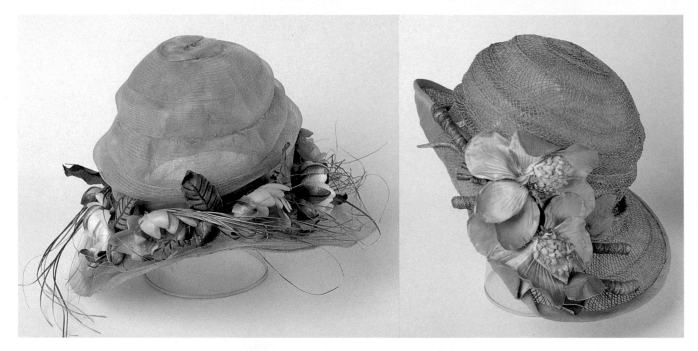

pellers, and pin bolts. A scarf tied like a propeller completed the outfit.

The fad for the dented helmet/ cloche began to wind down within the year. "Smart women no longer appear like members of a regiment wearing uniform felt hats. Standardization is démodé," preached a *Vogue* editorial. The hat remained clochelike, but it was a cloche that roguishly exposed the face. "Women are allowed to have eyebrows, or at least one, by day, as well as night" was the new rule of thumb. Brims shrank, or performed acrobatics—slashed, rolled, and twisted in front to show the brow. The creases and pinches of the crown shifted from the brim to the body of the hat and back again, creating fantastically sculpted shapes. Turbans, skullcaps, and toques were also part of the vocabulary, replacing the cloche.

Merchants and millinery manufacturers must have been thrilled when the cloche fell out of fashion, since it had commercial drawbacks. Women

Although the "popover" hat, like the model, **OPPOSITE ABOVE**, was popular, women still had a soft spot for pretty picture hats, such as the early 1920s horsehair (or crin) hat, **ABOVE LEFT**, with cotton flowers and grasses, which measures 29 inches in circumference (label: Paul Poiret). The natural-colored openwork straw hat, brimmed at front and sides, **ABOVE RIGHT**, is a sister style. A sportier version with stitched trim, is **OPPOSITE BELOW**.

could return felt cloches to their milliners, season after season, to be cleaned, reblocked, and recut. Recycling a hat was no style crime.

Meanwhile, the big, droopy-brimmed chapeau flourished side by side with the cloche. These formal hats were larger than street hats, the choice for garden parties, the beach, and the flowing dresses of spring and summer. In contrast to the generally subdued palette of the tailored cloche, picture hats appeared in gorgeous peacock colors that complemented the dress.

The same softly draped quality characterized the "gigolo," which looked like a female version of the man's fedora. A Paris original, the gigolo had a small brim that turned up in the back and down in front, and a high crown with a center crease. The absolute standard for 1926, the gigolo moved *Vogue*'s Paris correspondent to yawn that it appeared "so often that one believed the members of a school or an institution must be passing by." The no-nonsense gigolo was matched with practical, sports-style day wear: pleated skirts, long plain jackets. In the evening, the flapper abandoned her restraint to flounce in dresses constructed with yokes, ruffles, panels, and gathers at hips, waist, or back. This drapery made its mark on millinery too, launching the use of fabrics that were easily manipulated—velvet, lamé, velour, and knitted jersey.

Fashion was also complicated by the arrival of color-coordinated dressing. Although the idea had surfaced a few years earlier, it only became an unbreakable rule in 1926. Bags, shoes, hats, scarves—even muffs, parasols, and corsages—were matched by color or material. Another innovation was the use of two and three colors on hats, handbags, even shoes. The chapeau matched or contrasted with the dominant color of the dress or coat. The end of World War I inspired a craving for color: shocking tango orange, orchid, sulphur yellow, and tarragon green—alone or in jolting combinations—added the gift of their vividness to clothing and accessories. In 1925, following the Exposition des Arts Décoratifs in Paris, a bright mix of "modernistic" and "Cubist" colors became stylish, often used together in triangular patches. Milliners picked up the theme, fashioning hats from geo-

metric print fabrics; even painting or embroidering ribbons to match.

Although a fresh color palette was introduced every season, the black hat was the wardrobe workhorse for the 1920s. It was the chapeau equivalent of the classic "little black dress." "All the dictates of the world's modists could not force the smart woman to sacrifice the becoming black hat without which she considers her wardrobe incomplete," nodded the *Dry Goods Economist* in 1928. In 1929, *Vogue* declared black millinery to be the indisputable choice of the superior Parisian woman, further explaining that the French milliners offered "gay colors" only for "overseas buyers."

When suntanning became chic late in the decade, "suntanesque" shades of beige, toast, café-au-lait, nude, and

off-white became fashion's new neutrals, especially for sportswear.

The nearly unlimited assortment of millinery materials was limited only by the months they could be worn. For example: for January and February

1925, satin was acceptable. For March and April, there were straws, raffia, and sheer printed silks. To be worn in May and June were exotic straws, lace, and chintz. The July and August selection included satin, velvet, and felt. Velvet and hatter's plush were for September and October; fur fabrics and fur, suede, velvet, felt, and lamé cloth finished the millinery year in November and December.

In 1929, *Vogue* looked back over the past few years and observed that 75 percent of the smart hats were felt. Felt wasn't just plain felt: a versatile material, it could be as hairy as fur, matte as crepe, lustrous as panne. It could be patterned with an overlay, stamped, carved, painted, and burned. Felt was also a good mixer, teamed with everything from velvet to silk to straw. Dyed in a variety of pastel col-

ors, it was even worn in the summer.

During the winter months, fur predominated. Flat furs—goat, broadtail, and karakul—were millinery signatures, matched to fur coats. While all-fur hats were worn, such as sable turbans and beaver berets, it was preferred as a trim; ermine tails and mink pompons were favorites. Supple doe, kidskin, and suede hats were common, sometimes paired with a corsage of the same material. The straightforward approach was occasionally supplemented with an oddball combination. In 1920,

crepe, taffeta, moiré, and silk—plain, lacquered, or embossed. In keeping with the 1920s' fascination with metallics, millinery used gold, silver, and

> By 1929, hats copied the severe bobbed hairdo. The satin helmet with pink silk inserts, **OPPOSITE**, is made without any stiffening or support, a far cry from the old-fashioned picture hat, **BELOW**, of ruched silk taffeta with a beaded medallion (attributed to Jeanne Lanvin, about 1922).

cheted of straw, cellophane, Visca, raffia, and ribbon.

Off and on during the decade, sports and daytime hats were trimless and low key, set off with a plain ribbon band or other minor garnish. Evening hats, and the fancy, formal cartwheels of spring and summer, knew no bounds. They were enriched with a wealth of detail, a reflection of fashion's decorative mania. With no shortage of skilled cheap labor, handwork included intricate beading, smocking, sashes and wrapping, appliqué, em-

a photographer captured the Russian ballerina Anna Pavlova in a chunky-looking, mousquetaire-shaped fur hat draped with a finely embroidered lace veil. Suzanne Talbot's 1928 creation was a close-fitting black ponyskin helmet, garnished with a mesh veil.

Extravagant, luxurious fabrics counteracted the simplicity of the hat. The vocabulary was endless—satin, faille,

opalescent lamé, tulles, and laces. Brocade and tapestry were the elegant heavyweights.

For hot weather and resort wear, a handful of straws were described as "regulation": bangkok, ballibuntl, milan, leghorn, and panama. Following the sportswear-propelled interest in knit clothing that developed in the mid-1920s, hats were knit and cro-

broidery, and hand-painting. Faux flowers, fruit, foliage, and vegetables were wreathed around brims, or put to work as a solo garnish. Feather fancies ranged from whole birds to parts of birds to feathers, used as cascades, sunbursts, tassels, pinwheels.

The hatpin rode along with the new importance of costume jewelry, recently created under the couturier's

loid. Like jewelry, these were small-scale ornaments: figures and animals in enameled metal, monograms set with diamonds, abstract spikes and bars inlaid with tortoise.

What went up in the early 1920s came down in 1928, as hemlines and hairstyles responded to gravity and fashion's whim. Longer dresses (four inches below the knee for day, six inches or floor-dusting for evening) were better—and more aerodynamically correct. According to *Fashionable Dress,* "The new silhouette in women's clothes harmonizes with the long streamline of the last made automobile, or the winged grace of the airplane." Bobbed hair lacked this flowing line; it looked too abrupt. The style that replaced it was longer, and smoothly waved close to the head. To cover up the bob's awkward growing-out stage, the latest Paris chapeaux were long in back. The towering, one-

eye-baring, brimmed helmet gave way to a snug hat with "ears" that drooped behind the head. The effect was like a deflated Mickey Mouse cap.

Evening ensembles exhibited a mature new sophistication: heads were swathed in tulle or sheer chiffon turbans; dresses boasted long sleeves, after years of sleevelessness; furs and corsets were favored. This elegance became the signal look for the 1930s. The flapper—with her short hair and short skirts—was finished, replaced by the cool gentility of "ladylike" types. Just before the stock market crash, *Fashionable Dress* bid the flapper adieu:

> She has exhausted the piquant claim of short skirts which used to swing to and fro in important little jerks. The lady has come back into style. But remember, it is no ordinary lady. It is a lady who was once a flapper and who is both disarmingly frank, yet seductive. . . . Life is certainly going to be interesting.

Supple drapery was a notable development late in the decade. The silent film star Pola Negri took full advantage of its sultry effect, **ABOVE**. A picture hat with a draped crown is another example of the trend, **OPPOSITE**. The Dolly Sisters, Parisian-based dancers, model matching wide-brimmed hats sashed beneath the chin, **BELOW**.

label. Frequently matched to a brooch, hatpins ran the gamut of materials from rhinestones to coral and cellu-

the **30s**

cocktails and
the seven dwarfs

Hats of the 1930s didn't inspire neutral opinions:
they were greeted with compliments, catcalls, and
complaints. Complaints were probably the most popular response. Society newspaper columnist Cholly
Knickerbocker called the headgear of his day a "lu-
nacy sweepstakes." A writer in *Esquire* magazine
proposed a conspiracy theory: unflattering hats were
a plot hatched by homosexual milliners to make
women look ridiculously unattractive to men.

If women have no wit *in* their heads
they have a right to wear somebody
else's witty concoctions *on* their
heads! —ELSA MAXWELL

Esquire could have laid the same shabby claim against fashion in general, since "pretty" had been conquered by "chic," with its toughly stylish, slightly erotic character. The 1930s fashionable woman wasn't a "gamine"—she was a "babe." Clothing—especially accessories—boasted an arrogantly humorous attitude, exemplified by Elsa Schiaparelli's work. Surrealism and even Walt Disney's cartoon character Grumpy made funky, piquant contributions to style. The international fairs and expositions put the native dress of North Africa, India, Asia, and South America into the spotlight. Hollywood, another exotic locale, made actresses from Joan Crawford to Mae West the models for millions of women. In addition to keeping up with contemporary sources, women practically had to hit the history books to follow fashion in the 1930s, as Paris couturiers and American designers yanked in everyone from Mary Stuart to Louisa May Alcott for inspiration.

The Delineator nailed down the philosophy: "Dress is merely the foundation stone on which [a woman] erects, with the hat, gloves, shoes, stockings, bag, flowers and jewels, a small but costly altar to chic."

Although exaggeration had its appeal, women tended to be more fearlessly outré with their accessories than with their clothing. Millinery took note. The monotonous reign of the cloche—dismissed by *Vogue* as "alike as two million peas"—was finished. What replaced it was a giddy parade of styles. Beginning around 1935, hats brandished spectacular trims, blinding colors, awe-inspiring, or just plain silly, shapes. Beaton ran up a laundry list:

> Bonnets, berets, sailors, Dolly Vardons, toques, homburgs, boaters, tammies, lancrets, marechaux, vagabonds, zouaves, Marinas, skullcaps, picture and Tyrolean hats—these are worn by the crowd. Felt hats, hard, bendy, matt and glossy hats, trimmed, untrimmed, moulded, draped, pink, navy-blue, and black.

While individuality reigned in hat styles, conformity still dictated their roles, which were left over from the 1920s: hats for morning, afternoon, evening, and sports. These categories gradually eased up, so that some sports hats went out in the afternoon, and evening hats saw daylight. In 1935, *Millinery Trade Review* acknowledged the hat's widening role, explaining that chic was "no longer a question of a hat for every dress—but one hat for five or six dresses."

To be truly on the cutting edge, that special "one hat" customarily carried a French label. The most notable Parisian milliners of the 1930s included Marie-Alphonsine, Agnès, Louise Bourbon, Rose Descat, Maria Guy, Reboux, and Suzy, as well as the hat-making couturiers Balenciaga, Coco Chanel, Lucien Lelong, Mainbocher, Edward Molyneux, and Jean Patou. However, American milliners also flexed their muscles: their work acquired a cachet that was equal to the Parisians'. Their ranks included Erik Braagard, John-Frederics, Lilly Daché, G. Howard Hodge, and Sally Victor.

The 1930s opened with the Depression and its poor-cousin attitude. "It is vulgar to be rich and extravagant. Even if you haven't lost money, you must pretend you have," was Cecil Beaton's artfully dodging analysis. Even Chanel bowed to necessity, creating evening dresses of cotton piqué.

If a new outfit wasn't in the budget, accessories did the job of boosting spirits. Chirped *Fashion Arts,* "Hats are more hilarious than ever this year. If they don't banish the Depression, nothing will."

One Depression vanquisher was Schiaparelli's "madcap," a small and shapeless knit tube that could be pulled into any shape by the wearer. A huge international hit, the madcap was widely copied, made up in linen, silk, wool, Visca, or chenille. A few seasons later, the stretch or knit hat was universal. Bonnets, berets, drapable hoods, tams, and turbans were knit or crocheted for the first time in yarn enhanced with stretchable rubber Lastex. Knit crowns were teamed with brims of stitched linen, straw, or felt. They were either handmade, custom-knit to order

> Hats took a precarious tilt in the 1930s. An angled grosgrain chapeau with a bountiful bow, **PAGE 30,** was inspired by the masculine top hat, and the astrakhan caps (by Talbot), **ABOVE,** by the Empress Eugénie. Even straw was draped and folded into shape, **OPPOSITE.**

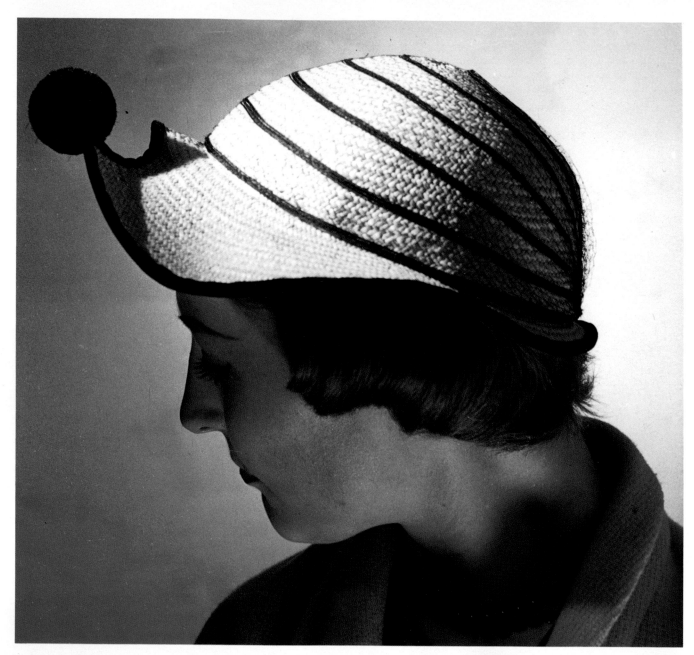

by department stores, or available readymade, priced from $1.00 to $3.95 for nondesigner brands. The rag knit hat was a novelty because of its material—and its role: it was equally chic for sport or town. As an example of the way these hand-knits had broken formal fashion rules, there was Schiaparelli's odd combination: she wore ropes of pearls, a crepe cape bordered with lush silver fox, and a pancake beret of simple white cotton string.

As the Depression began to lift toward the end of 1932, Plain Jane cotton gave way to the luxe of jewel-toned velvet, used for millinery, dresses, wraps, and coats; studded with rhinestones, it was made up into cravats, gloves, handbags, belts, and headgear. The wealthy woman could also enjoy "uncopyable elegance": a karakul beret by a Paris couturier, priced at an

The exaggerated silhouette was millinery's signature. A cap of straw, **ABOVE**, conquered a woman's profile and her hairdo. The dramatically structured felt hat, **OPPOSITE**, with brass hat pin (by Howard Hodge) appeared close to the end of the decade.

astounding—for the day—$125.

In 1931, a small felt hat, garnished with an ostrich feather, made a fierce debut. The "Empress Eugénie" dipped low over one eye, obscuring vision, and tilted up in back. Familiarly called the "EE," the hat was inspired by the riding topper of its namesake 19th-century empress, wife of Napoleon III.

Hysterically popular with women, the Eugénie hat was greeted with hysteria by men, who called it "a soup plate with a turned-up edge" that made women look as if they'd "been hit on the head with a hammer." "Profiles," mused *Vogue,* "have become more important than eyes." Other hats followed the Eugénie's asymmetrical look, so that for a year, the right side of a hat looked totally unrelated to its left. Veils, flowers, and feather fancies were also players in the cult of superfemininity of the Eugénie.

At its peak of popularity, an original Paris-made Eugénie beanie by Rose Valois or Agnès cost $45 at Best & Company in New York; the store copies were $15. (By comparison, a floor-length satin evening dress was priced at $39.50.) The Lava Soap radio program paid snide poetic tribute:

> Here's to the Princess Eugénie,
> That sits on the side of my beanie;
> My husband laughs,
> The big giraffe,
> Don't you think he's a meanie?

> Here's to the Princess Eugénie,
> Over one ear it does leanie;
> By covering one ear,
> Don't you see, my dear,
> You have only one ear to cleanie!

By 1932, "American women . . . recovered their sanity under the sturdy candor of American men," claimed *Fashion Accessories.* "The extreme Eugénie hat went the way of all epidemics."

In 1933, once Eugénie was finished, fashion introduced a less delicate female inspiration: Mae West. When her period film *She Done Him Wrong* opened in Paris, couturiers and

their clients took notice. A socialite, Madame Tréfusis, introduced Mae to society at a party on the terrace of the Eiffel Tower, and all the right crowd came in costumery that mimicked the movie star's, including wasp-waisted dresses and gigantic, feather-bordered chapeaux, circa 1910. Mae West, with her "big hats and her big ways, has superseded the Greta Garbo—Marlene Dietrich school," commented a magazine. Thanks to Mae, the skimpy coat-hanger silhouette was rounded out.

There were no startling style developments in 1933, and 1934 was only slightly more exceptional. Elsa Schiaparelli's collection in 1933 was typically all over the map: for spring, she did cowboy brimmers, crowns, Phrygian bonnets, and pillboxes. Agnès's tall black satin chechia of 1933 came back in 1934 as the towering cossack hat. Faddish delicacies included Agnès's little skullcaps of silk ribbon frayed to look like a thatch of unruly hair, in colors that matched or contrasted with the wearer's own curls.

Although no one millinery attitude dominated in 1934, the tricky crown, shoved every which way, was a hallmark: it came tucked, folded, sloped forward, backward, upward. A wonder-

"The chic severity of a costume is pointed up with a piece of barbaric jewelry, a silly looking hat," counseled the magazine editors of *Style* in 1935. A high-pointed witch hat of the 1930s, made of felt, **RIGHT**, ranked in the silly category, but there were many examples of *outré,* albeit stylish, millinery as seen in the illustrations, **OPPOSITE**, from the 1938 season.

ful example was the "Scap cap," Schiaparelli's saucy little dunce cap, in velvet, faille, or felt; its pointed top was folded down and fastened with a safety pin, tassel, or bow.

Brims went narrow or shot straight up in back (mousquetaire style), or even rolled up all the way around (sombrero style). Brims stuck out like baseball visors, shovels, and boat prows. For spring, Schiaparelli created a hat with a pleated all-the-way-around brim, of knitted blue rayon. Mainbocher's huge-brimmed felt and velvet chapeaux were turned up and feathered on the left side, cavalier style. Curiously, he showed them with floor-length dresses. Size wasn't the only novel appeal of the cartwheels: these braggadocio hats were worn in daylight, with strict tailleurs.

Vogue described the effect— "One's body . . . should be a narrow stem, one's head sleek and shiny and small—topped off by an immense, stiff, straight hat." At the same time, they acknowledged that the big hat was "nothing to dive in and out of the subways with." In Paris, luggage makers happily filled orders for trunks that could hold four to six of these cartwheel monsters, which could measure 17 inches across. In summer, old-fashioned gingham and overscale straw bonnets hit the beach.

Width took yet another direction with the beret. The beret stretched out of its traditional scale, growing to mammoth size, embellished with visors, peaks, turned-up brims, swooping high in back and low in front. Rose Descat offered berets in 57 varieties in a single season. *Harper's Bazaar* antic-

enhanced) and satin were made up into headwear for day and night, with handbags, gloves, belts, and scarves.

There was a less flexible reaction to millinery beginning in 1935; howls of disbelief and moans of complaint failed to turn women from their stylish pursuit. The goal was to look "smart." The post-Prohibition revival of the cocktail hour called for snappy, uncompromising new hattery, and women did the occasion proud.

For inspiration, fashion stole from history and foreign countries. Clothes were "calculated to confuse the merchant and strike terror into the cus-

> By 1932, the side-tipped chapeau was no longer chic. It was replaced by the hat that sat squarely on the head. Sitting straight, **OPPOSITE**, is a woven straw topper, pinched into a bicorne. Another fashion directional, **ABOVE LEFT** and **BELOW RIGHT**, was "never look static." Hats were pushed back or pushed forward, which gave the impression of action, accentuated here by the illustrator's rendition of a windy day.

tomer, who saw herself in turn, an Italian primitive, a Greek Venus, a Hindu Nautch dancer and any number of other things," noted *Fashion's Art*. Coaxed the *Junior League Bulletin*, "Lose your nationality as soon as night falls." Grecian drapery was worn in the evening with gold sandals, eye shadow, and nail polish. A "Hindoo" style (saris and Turkish trousers) was conjured up by Alix and Schiaparelli.

Ersatz turbans accompanied this exotica. Towering, cone-shaped nests of brocade, metal-shot crepe, metal cloth, velvet, or batik, they were twisted, folded, pleated, or shirred into

position. Turbans were for wearing in late afternoon and evening, a chic choice for velvet-trimmed wool ensembles. In real life, turbanned maharajas and maharanis jammed Paris on their way to London for George V's Jubilee, traveling with 300 trunks apiece. Their saris "almost outnumbered the made-in-Paris variety," cracked *Vogue*.

Beginning mid-decade, other events—the threat of war in Europe and the revival of Abel Gance's epic silent film *Napoleon*—received credit for the *mode militaire*. Soldierly details adorned clothing: soutache, braid, frog closures, epaulets, brass buttons, and velvet and fur trim. Hats were also possessed by the martial spirit, bristling with rosettes, tassels, pompons, feather cockades, and braid. Napo-

ipated their readers' reaction to this with a yawn: "She is getting a little sick of it, but she wears it just the same. It is much bigger than last year's . . . squashed forward over one eye."

When gold was devalued, it became fashion's preoccupation: lamé evening bags, gold sandals, costume jewelry, massive gold bracelets, and hefty bead necklaces from Cartier. Even sports clothes were weighted with golden threads. Milliners responded with turbans of glittery woolens, lamés, and metal cloth. Jeanne Lanvin's evening hat, for example, was a Crusader's turban of tulle studded with paillettes.

Another example of fashion's about-face: classic evening fabrics crossed over into day wear. All types of velvet (silk, artificial, and elastic Lastex-

leon-inspired tricornes, bicornes, quadricornes, and Citizen Jacobin caps—souvenirs of the French Revolution—were back. Lilly Daché did Palace Gate guard hats. Agnès created pointed soldier caps exactly like the kind children make from folded paper. Fur cossack caps, a holdover from 1933, made another showing.

Another influence was drawn from a native theme: the American dude ranch. Surprisingly, the redoubtable Chanel even picked up on this mode, creating nail-studded belts and bandannas. Molyneux resurrected the Davy Crockett and Daniel Boone fur caps—complete with dangling tails—to accessorize afternoon ensembles.

For a less colloquial inspiration, milliners haunted the springtime Exposition de l'Art Italien, held at the Petit Palais in Paris, and the Exposition of Flemish Art at the Tuileries. Falling into their own Renaissance revival, they created unabashed copies of the hats in the paintings. Agnès and Schiaparelli favored the skullcaps of Dante and Petrarch. Agnès also created a series of draped berets plus her trademark color, "Agnès blue," the exact sapphire purple shade of Gothic stained glass. (True blue to fashion, Agnès and her showroom mannequins also tinted their hair a lighter shade of the same color.)

Rich velvets were the materials of the Renaissance headgear. Veronese's vibrant green, ruby, Titian rose, bronze, and malachite rivaled the popularity of the ubiquitous black hat. "I sell four colored hats to one black," bragged Lilly Daché in 1935. An often violent color contrast (both hats and

Mid-decade, millinery offered up a smorgasbord of styles. A wool felt hat, **ABOVE LEFT**, shows a Napoleonic influence (label: Albany). A heavy mesh swathes a pointed straw topper (label: Made to order by John-Frederics), **ABOVE RIGHT**. Daisies circled a brim on the hat matched to a dress from Nicole de Paris, **OPPOSITE ABOVE**, and a Hollywood hat featured a wrapped crown, **OPPOSITE BELOW**.

accessories) was a hallmark that year. *Millinery Trade Review* noted that 80 percent of spring millinery was blue, often with peony pink decoration. Many were sailor hats, garnished with crisp pleats, ribbons, or all-out frills, and worn straight on the head; those

with a forward-jutting brim were tipped at an angle. Enamored of the sailor, Molyneux made it with double brims, such as felt with gleaming cellophane on a straw crown.

Side by side with the neat sailors were the monster cartwheels, still news after their popularity in 1934. This time around, the cartwheel was even more exaggerated, sometimes as wide as a parasol, done up in light or rough-textured straw. Some cartwheels were just brims, with a draped handkerchief or veil serving as a crown.

Dresses were giddy confections of net, silk, and cotton ruffles in sugary colors. The addition of fabric flowers transformed women into portable gardens, to the point of comic exaggeration: gardenias were strapped across bare backs, wreathed around wrists and the waist. Corsages were the size of bouquets. Blooms accented every type of hat from turbans to sailors; Patou even matched the print on his dresses to the flowers on his hats.

Contemporary Modes magazine claimed veiling was more in demand in 1935 than it had been in the last 20 years, used on all but sports hats.

Reboux's black antelope hat had an arsenic-green Chantilly lace veil; two-toned veils (wine and navy, green and rust) swathed other hats, bow-tied under the chin. Informal veils were stiff, large-meshed net; finer, dressier types were bordered in sequins, or chenille embroidery (arabesques, dots), fastened on with jeweled clips. Schiaparelli launched hairnets of pearls, gold, silver, or brilliant jet. She also revived the *résille* (a coarse-meshed chenille snood) that fit over the hair in back, topped with a narrow cap.

Ostrich feathers were another glamorous revival. There were knobbly tips,

sprays, brushes, sunbursts, *touffes,* tassels, swaggering torsades, pompons, and flat-leaf and flower-shaped forms. There were flat-pasted wings. Full, drooping shower arrangements. Feather bands that climbed the brim.

Fur, feathers, and flowers continued to reign as head-to-toe ornament, as economics improved. "The Depression's over," cheered *Contemporary Modes* in 1936. "Let's dress up." Flowers were still rampant on clothing and headgear, blanketing the bodices of evening dresses, covering sleeves, even skirts; Schiaparelli's white chiffon gown was completely overgrown with yellow mimosas. Purple was fashion's color of choice, and grapes wreathed décolletage, hats, and

heads. Flowers and feathers adorned new chignons and tight curls. In France pieces of birds—or the entire creature—perched on hats; real stuffed birds were forbidden in America. Miles of veiling swathed heads. Handwork included embroidery, echoing the Tyrolean influence.

Fur had the same exaggerated treatment. Generous amounts of the stuff were put to use as trim, and fashioned into all-fur chapeaux. Leopard was the animal of choice, prowling into millinery along with black Persian lamb and gray astrakhan. Though not fresh news, the fur cossack cap was still around. With fur hats, there were dresses inset with fur, jackets with furred backsides, and skirts with fur aprons or pockets. The accessories included Persian

lamb, and ermine gloves and muffs of silver fox, sable, or mink, which replaced handbags.

The derby was the year's masculine incarnation; fashion magazines traced its ancestry to Henry II and the Second Empire, and they credited its 1936 incarnation to Schiaparelli. Schiap's version came in felt or straw; a length of veil was tossed over the hat and tied under the chin. The bold derby complemented her edgy, masculine suits with square padded shoulders.

By 1936, the Near Eastern—inspired turban mutated into a strange configuration. Agnès did a tall, turbanesque cone hat in black antelope, inset with green and violet bands. Schiaparelli promoted Phrygian toques. The Parisian milliner Suzy went one better: her black velvet dunce cap was stabbed through each side with two long and stiff green quills, pointing in opposite directions.

Martinique was another source for the exotica of 1936. Following native example, there were bandanna-style turbans, draped from brightly striped or patterned silk or chiffon madras. Also under the Martinique label were shoulder-wide cartwheels and upturned, towering fruit-basket straws.

A brand new silhouette was inaugurated. Louise Bourbon and Le Monnier both engineered a hat with a pillbox front; in the back, it curved down to cover the head flatly, extending almost to the nape of the neck. Berets were still in the picture, as huge floppy toppers, or even slabs of felt that looked like newspaper-boy gear.

Though the turban continued, it proceeded without the metallic fabric that had been its signature. Felt, velvet, and antelope were the most common materials for 1936; felt and velvet were a favorite, doubled-up.

Clashing color, which had made a minor appearance in 1935, was now in full force—notably Schiaparelli's hot, shocking pink. Pairing two contrasting colors was common, as in Robert Piquet's frock, which was rust in front and navy in back. Hats followed the same scheme, scrambling together two and three colors and fabrics: violet with black, or lime plus brown. The unusual palette made for wonderful copy. Coughed *Vogue,* "If you are taking a lady out to lunch and find that she arrives with white eyelids and green eyelashes don't let off a piercing scream and telephone for an ambulance. . . . It's her new way of making herself interesting."

In 1937, headwear topped even the outlandish models of the year before. Milliners abandoned all historical references, turning to such offbeat inspirations as milk cans, duck bills, and bread baskets. The results defied description. At the hands of Schiaparelli and Jean Patou, headwear took on daring size and gnomish shapes reminiscent of the Seven Dwarfs. Toques were coiled, draped, built to stand by any possible means, following no rules of

In the mid-1930s, milliners used velvet to create very different looks: a bonnet equipped with streamers (label: Bergdorf Goodman), **ABOVE**, and a toque in two-toned velvet, draped with a mantilla-like veil, **OPPOSITE**.

material or construction. *Harper's Bazaar* gave this millinery an acrobatic character: "rising like crags, shelving into eaves of felt, shooting out wildly at rabid angles, sprouting ostrich, ducking to chin straps, doing things they never did before."

The art movement Surrealism also contributed a fair share of inspiration, credited with the most notorious piece of millinery, Schiaparelli's shoe hat. Agnès's felt topper that zipped apart at the seams was another jarring, slightly sinister whimsy.

Schiaparelli's hats for warm weather were equally exceptional, made from real straw bread baskets filled with long-stemmed fabric roses or pansies. Chanel chalked up her high hats to women's stature, proclaiming, "A woman is a little thing beside a man . . . therefore, since I don't care for evening hats, I have made these headdresses to give her height, to make her more of a person, more important." Her height-giving headdresses were girlish—a hankie-sized bit of veiling anchored with roses, or a silk zinnia topknot with bows.

Meanwhile, the turban continued its evolution. According to *Vogue,* the Directoire Ball, held in the spring of 1937 in Paris, incited the turban frenzy. Female guests sported turbans created by Suzy, Reboux, or Agnès: twisted towers of lamé, suede, or velvet, jabbed with ostrich feathers. Real jewels were pinned in the center. A white jersey turban with a white jersey dress and gold jewelry was a summer classic.

Other foreign influences cast a spell. When President Franklin Roosevelt went to South America, fashion followed, offering Peruvian sombreros, chechias, and gaucho berets. The palette went tropical: colors such as Panama Coral, Mayan Blue, and Brazilian Orange were used solo, or in grating combinations. Even Chanel included gaudy, multicolored stripes in her col-

lection. Other couturiers fell in love with ''brick dust''—a color associated with the French Colonial Exposition.

''Decorative'' was fashion's operating word in 1937. Clothes were loaded with velvet and fur, jewels and metal ornaments; sequins and embroidery echoed the lavishness of Louis XV. Hat trimmings were just as bravura, ranging from braid to fringe to fur pompons. A tall bow, placed center front, was a millinery signature. A harvest of other oddball trim novelties included acorns, fruits, vegetables, shells, and nuts. Veiling appeared in four lengths —eyelashes, nose, chin, belt buckle.

Although exaggeration had been the byword of fashion for several seasons, *Harper's Bazaar* made it official in the spring of 1938: ''We are entering a season when fashion is almost a fancy-dress party. When clothes must be lived up to, else there's no point in wearing them.''

One of the interpretations of fancy dress was the itsy-bitsy doll's hat, which debuted that spring. Men detested it. ''If the male populace had reason to direct jibes at last season's millinery,'' sighed the *Millinery Trade Review,* ''there will now be reason to continue the motion.'' The *New York Sunday Mirror* called the doll's hat ''the entire gamut of female cussedness reduced and confined to a few spare inches of hat.'' Nevertheless, the hat was commemorated. When it came time to seal the quintessential 1930s topper into a copper time capsule at the New York World's Fair, the doll's hat was the natural choice. In 5,000 years, the capsule will be reopened to reveal a miniature green and purple hat decked out with a veil and purple ostrich feathers, a creation by Lilly Daché.

The year 1938 was one without rules. Milliners made crowns high and low, or shirred, draped, and tucked into shape. Robin Hood and the Wicked Witch gave their namesakes to hattery. There were giddy buccaneer hats, pinched peach baskets, sombreros, pie plates, Louis XIV tricornes. Picture and coolie hats mutated into mushroomlike silhouettes. Berets resembled collapsed muffins. Historical hat models included the periods 1900, the 1880s, and the 1890s. Muffs, veils, fans, and even crinoline-powered

The itsy-bitsy doll's hat—child-sized and worn by adults, such as the straw hat with plaid trim, **LEFT**—swept millinery in 1938. When Indian potentates visited London for the Coronation, turbans, like the example **ABOVE** (by Suzy), became wildly popular.

skirts were part of the look. The Persian Exposition launched a craze for Oriental colors, as well as the fez, the chechia, and the towering turban.

No matter what their shape, hats shared the same posture: tipped drunkenly forward. Hair was coiffed to match, pulled up into a forehead nest of permed curls, exposing the nape of the neck. To maintain the precarious tilt, bands and ribbons gripped hat and hair. An alternative was the topper with a kind of fitted "flap" over the back of the head to balance its forward slant. Scarves—like a variation on a Bedouin headdress—also kept hats in line. Louise Boulanger's dunce hat of panama sported a waist-length swath of green georgette. Pillboxes came with wimples. Ribbon-trimmed and tied hats were common, from Schiaparelli's sunbonnets to "halo" hats bow-tied under the chin.

Elsa Schiaparelli's October collection, modeled after the 18th-century commedia dell'arte, was promoted by American department stores. Her collection of mad hattery included mask hats, tricornes, oversized floppy berets, clown-painted dunce hats, a pillbox with a harlequin face in relief across the top. Walt Disney was a match for Schiap's whimsy. He licensed a line of Seven Dwarf hats from the movie *Snow White*. Happy's hat was a pointed gnome hat in delphinium-blue felt; Doc's pale-blue antelope topper had a slanting, cone-shaped crown.

The king and queen of England's visit to Paris in 1938 popularized Scotch plaid ribbons. "If all the ribbons used this season in Paris were

laid end to end, they would reach around the earth and leave enough to tie in an immense bow on the equator," imagined *Contemporary Modes*.

Other top trims included fur (bleached skunk, fox, leopard, polar bear, and even Mongolian wolf) and flora.

Meanwhile, an ominous shadow fell over Paris: hatlessness. The alarmed response to this threat was an indication of the hat's entrenchment as a social standard. *Harper's Bazaar* ridiculed the Parisian "hatless ones" as "half decapitated creatures" who appeared to be not quite dressed, giving the appearance of "escaping [the] wrath of their husbands—running out on a family row." Though hatlessness was never widespread at this time, it

presaged the bareheaded style that would flourish during the war.

In the tense interim period before war was declared, fashion had its own kind of precarious balance. Dresses were backed with bustles, waists were pinched by corsets, and bonnets pitched forward or backward on the head. The desired millinery effect was what *Vogue* described as "a heavy flower on a frail stem." The doll's hat

Feathers were key in the romantic revival: a foam of ostrich feathers could become a chapeau, **OPPOSITE**. Extreme hats, like the one **BELOW**, were the target for jokes. Hard-edged hats also held their own, such as the pointed asymmetrical stitched wool hat (label: Henri Bendel), **RIGHT**.

—no longer known by that name—survived by gaining weight (veiling draped from brim to shoulders) or adding height (15-inch feathers poised at attention, warbonnet style).

The extreme silhouettes of the previous year continued: sugarloaf shapes, kettles, towering crowns. Lampshades, peach baskets, boats, and bowls were millinery's tongue-in-cheek terms for hats with no historical precedents.

And veiling: the year 1939 was wound around with miles of it—fine, coarse, embroidered, spangled with sequins, decked with flowers. "Swath your head and shoulders in mists of veiling, and determine whether they give you allure or make you look as if you were going to raid a beehive," counseled *Vogue*. It was a further triumph of exaggeration that veil was even tied over veil, the colors blurring together. Veils descended to preposterous new lengths: actress Dorothy Lamour wore a tiny black hat draped with a red-dotted veil as long as her skirt.

Snoods were part of the veiling and drapery story. One magazine published some statistics: in one shop, 80 percent of the hats sold had snoods; in another, 26,000 snoods were sold in a

The decorative urge was irresistible, as in the straw picture hat, **OPPOSITE**, which boasts a band of costume jewels (label: Lilly Daché). Millinery trim included everything imaginable, from fur to knickknacks. With so many choices, the seasonal visit to the milliner, **BELOW**, became even more important. Each hat was matched to the client's wardrobe and custom-fitted in the shop.

nery'' included white plumes brushed with luminous paint, glow-in-the-dark ribbons, and even tiny glass flowers illuminated by means of a battery concealed under the crown. (By day, the flowers had a phosphorescent glow.)

Sensing a ''last fling,'' fashion laid on the screwball humor. Gloves had a built-in compartment for matches, handbags had built-in music boxes

season. Exotically colored fishnets were wrapped into turbans on the head. Sheer and printed jerseys, silks, and chiffons were worn as wimples, often matched to a dress.

With the approach of war, millinery became more and more minimal. In Paris, the milliner Suzy complained to

Contemporary Modes that her clients replaced their afternoon and evening hats with embroidered veils, and went hatless in the morning. To keep her customers from defecting, she created luminous floral hair ornaments to be worn during blackouts. Other designers' contributions to ''blackout milli-

that played when open, pockets had padlock closures. In the same spirit, ''everything but the kitchen sink''— from plastic dogs. to dangling heart pins—sprouted on millinery. Enormous ribbons and flowers reared atop hats. As war cast a dark cloud, fashion made an exit, laughing.

the 40s

making do makes way for elegance

During wartime, women were quick-change artists, adept at performing an about-face. Carmel Snow, editor of *Harper's Bazaar,* identified this turnabout: "Women who themselves spend their days in uniforms, or grease-smeared coveralls, are particularly eager to look helpless and feminine and lovely, once their working hours are over." Even after working hours, however, patriotism was a 24-hour-a-day job. Magazines made some adjustments; home canning

As a result of the war and uniforms, women still looked and dressed like Amazons. But I designed clothes for flowerlike women, with rounded shoulders, full feminine busts, and hand-span waists above enormous spreading skirts. —CHRISTIAN DIOR

recipes were featured along with high fashion in *Harper's Bazaar.* The rest of the magazine skimped along, proud to present the logistics of "making do." Women wore colored leg makeup instead of nylons, joined a waiting list for black lingerie, sported costume jewelry crafted of pumpkin seeds, carried face powder in wooden compacts. While "do without" restricted beauty routines, there was one thing the 1940s gal had aplenty: character. *Mademoiselle* admiringly described her: "She'll be the wide-awake girl, the world-beater, the cheerful cherub, the season's slickeroo."

American fashion had the chance to show the same do-it-alone spunk, as couture went into isolation for the war's duration. In 1940, *Vogue* and *Harper's Bazaar* put their autumn issues to press without a single garment from Paris. French *Vogue* even ceased publication.

Enter American fashion, made up of equal parts Hollywood design and patriotism. There was a real hands-on-

Before war restrictions, millinery savored the lavish use of materials. A yard-long chiffon scarf graces a felt toque, **PAGE 52.** During the war, fabric flowers were an unrestricted bright note. **RIGHT.**

hips, "we'll show 'em" attitude about native-made styles. "American women are the best dressed in the world," bragged *Collier's.* "They can get good-looking clothes at any price they want to pay anywhere in the country. They can get them from a mail-order house if there isn't a store handy to the ranch." It's no wonder that *Annie Get*

Your Gun was a Broadway sensation.

Clothes that worked through the war obeyed the government's War Production Board L-85 ruling, which limited certain materials, including silk, wool, and leather. To conserve fabric, pleated skirts and French cuffs were forbidden, women's jackets could measure no longer than 25 inches, and

pockets were abbreviated. American designers coped admirably, creating suits with a narrow, straight, and reedy silhouette, popularized by Hollywood designer Adrian. A less severe model with a peplum and a gently flared skirt was also a favorite option.

Anything that smacked of peasant and Indian sources was patriotic, such

as moccasins, crocheted shawls, pleated "broomstick" skirts, and Mexican silver jewelry. *Mademoiselle* also noted other inspirations for the American woman's dress. "She'll have loyalties to neighborly nations that lead her to Chinese hairdos, Grecian draperies, screaming South American colors, and British Ambulance Corps prints." Loyalties also extended to products with foreign associations, like Coty's Warm Tamale makeup, Revlon's Chilibean nail polish, and rum-and-coke cocktails.

Accessories were another story: they were loud, colorful, and aggressive wardrobe stretchers. Handbags grew into enormous, unconstructed pillows, nearly identical to the muffs that were also brandished. Intricate handmade

detailing made up for the lack of first-class materials. Hats, gloves, veils, scarves, and even shoes were ornamented with nonrestricted sequins, spangles, and beads. Jewelry took the cartoons as inspiration; the materials shortage created resourceful solutions.

As for millinery, the Easter bonnet held a certain innocent magic; in 1940, 22 percent of yearly hat sales were made in March and April. "Saks Fifth Avenue's Mr. Joseph is not one to fly in the face of the tradition calling for freshness that amounts to impertinence in spring hats," observed writer

Lois Long in *The New Yorker*.

Despite Mr. Joseph's antics, most women shied away from the bizarre hattery of the late 1930s. Kooky and overly quaint hats fell from favor because they weren't male bait. *Vogue* counseled women for the return of their men from war: "The way not to look this year is hard, sharp, cold, even bold. It's out because the men can't bear it. The new hats are not crazy, zany, don't-let-your-husband-see-it hats . . . they are the Lady Hats."

Even with the advance of the Lady Hat, the less-than-a-lady chapeau persisted. As a male observer explained in *Collier's*:

There is much to be said about women's hats, and some of it can even be printed.

But probably the most vital thing that you can say about them is that they are designed to attract men. Most men either fail to realize this, or take sadistic delight in using the knowledge to abuse the ladies' choice. They have referred to women's chapeaux as aviaries, chicken roosts, jamons, pancakes, kellies, and Holy Joes.

Apparently the hat-as-beau-catcher concept was lost on women, who selected their headgear with an entirely different intent. According to *Contemporary Modes*, "To the ladies, a hat is a decorative affair designed to complete the ensemble, flatter the face, look newer than the one just bought by one's best friend."

During the war, the ladies and their friends had a hard time of it, as millinery distinguished itself more by ingenuity than stylishness. Without Paris, without the influence of the foreign fairs and expositions, and with materials rationing, American millinery suffered from a shortage of fresh ideas. The sober headwear of the early 1940s failed to measure up to the individuality that characterized the late 1930s.

Vogue introduced millinery for fall 1942 as having "character, consideration, distinction, and no daftness." That was an accurate but hardly an inspirational description. Fashion magazines glossed over millinery's lack of direction by presenting it as a new

A two-foot-wide velvet platter was a match for a severe suit (label: Lilly Daché), **ABOVE RIGHT**. A narrower hat gets the road test before an audience, **RIGHT**. A topper made of net (label: Howard Hodge) is inspired by menswear, **OPPOSITE**.

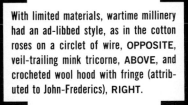

With limited materials, wartime millinery had an ad-libbed style, as in the cotton roses on a circlet of wire, OPPOSITE, veil-trailing mink tricorne, ABOVE, and crocheted wool hood with fringe (attributed to John-Frederics), RIGHT.

freedom. "Individuality stalks the head. Do what you like," shrugged *Harper's Bazaar*.

Fitting the definition of "individual" were the hand-knits: practical not pretty, they were one of the few wartime innovations. Clothing and accessories—from millinery to costume jewelry—were all needle-made. Whether commercially produced or fashioned at home, hand-knits were bulky, simply shaped, and slightly awkward. Both the making and the wearing of these knits was a patriotic gesture. They suited the early 1940s winter wardrobe, when keeping warm

was a primary objective. A typical cold-weather outfit might include clompy wooden-soled shoes, pants of fur-blend fabric, thick felt skirts, sloppy joe sweaters, knit boleros, and crocheted shawls. Even Hollywood sophisticates took hand-knits to their hearts. Gloria Swanson was devoted to her brown-and-yellow striped stocking cap and matching mittens. The decade's pinup, Lana Turner, was a "sweater girl."

Life magazine published a service feature on made-at-home hats in 1942. "*Life* editors are well aware that the strategy of hatmaking has as many

pitfalls as the strategy of invasion," was the sobering explanation given along with the instructions. Nevertheless, if a woman followed the step-by-step details, she could create 13 hats for $10, using buckram, flowers, and ribbons from the five-and-dime.

The wrapped head was one of the few novel styles developed in the early 1940s, though it was rooted in the late 1930s. One of the last hats flown out of Paris was the milliner Paulette's white hemp cloth turban, trailing a chiffon scarf that tied around the neck. The hat-with-a-scarf stayed in play, and in 1941, a year later, John-

Martha O'Driscoll

...raine Day

Carole
Landis

Marjorie
Reynolds

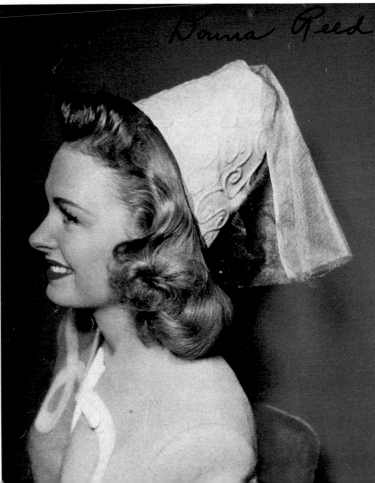

Donna Reed

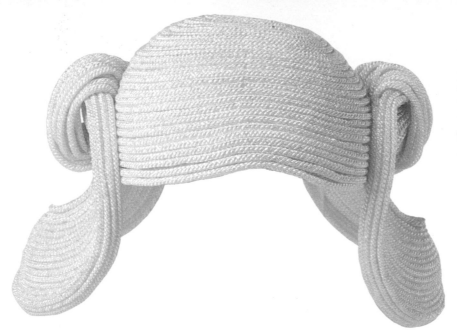

The wrapped head was a 1940s signature: a sleek wrapped straw hat of 1948 (label: Sally Victor), **LEFT**; and a silk jersey turban (label: Mme. Pauline, New York City), **BELOW**. In 1944 a swirl of satin ribbons (by Tatiana du Plessix of Saks Fifth Avenue), **OPPOSITE**, displayed a glamorous version of drapery in the pages of *Vogue*.

Frederics did a flat hat woven of panama straw, worn smashed down over a cerise silk scarf, wrapped tightly around the head. As a variation, scarves were also pulled over the hat, covering up all but half of the brim.

Cotton was another humble material put to use when milliners ran short of fancier supplies. Kerchiefs and scarves, twisted into turbans, were one of the last styles promoted in Paris before the German Occupation. Elsa Schiaparelli engineered turbans from cotton, raw silk, and silk stocking jersey for her autumn collection, shown in the spring of 1940.

For the winter of 1942, there were "capots," inspired by the Victorian originals. Kerchief-like, they tied on over the head, wrapped around the throat, and tied in front or back. A matching muff was the accompani-

A line-up of Hollywood stars celebrated the range of headgear available in 1940, **PAGES 60–61.**

ment. The 1940s capots were stiffened with crinoline, which shaped them to a more sophisticated fit than a kerchief. A model from Lilly Daché was made up in black broadcloth and edged with mink or braid. For evening, there were capots of beaded velvet and crepe.

The scarf technique led to new abandon in veiling, which was thrown

over hats to tie under the chin, swagged under the chin from ear to ear, or stretched snugly over the face. Making up for millinery's lack of manipulated details, veil ornamentation was unrestricted: it was beaded, spangled, strewn with leaves and blossoms. Some spring hats amounted to little more than a swarm of confetti-dotted netting.

After stockpiled supplies had been used up, there were shortages of lace, feathers, and silk. Certain types of metals and rubber for elastic were also restricted. However, there were enough alternative millinery decorations to brighten hats. Striped, checked, and plaid taffeta ribbons were popular, often matched with a scarf, gloves, or a handbag. Oddities such as upholstery fringe, cork, and shells were introduced as garnishes.

Straw imports from Italy ceased in 1940; milliners substituted raffia and starched cotton lace. Other materials had no ready substitutes. In 1940, a concoction of rabbit fur and skim milk produced a flat, thin type of felt. It wasn't enough. Two years later, the Wartime Production Board and the Fish and Wildlife Service urged an increase in the trapping of wild jack-

rabbits to relieve the domestically raised rabbit pelt shortage.

Both millinery and clothing followed the same pinchhitting approach for coping with material shortages, where an unrestricted fabric was teamed with a restricted type. A dress might have rayon sleeves and a wool bodice; a hat could mix precious fur felt with velvet.

Government regulations also forbade the use of some colors of dye. The colors that were available made for a wild palette. For example, redheaded comedienne Lucille Ball wore an eye-popping combo: a pale yellow frock wound with cummerbund of lime shad-ding to deep green, an orange fleece jacket, yellow accessories, and a hat trimmed with orange flowers.

If there was a single color that represented the war years, it would be luminescence. A serviceable as well as fashionable option were the blackout accessories, worn for greater visibility on dimmed-out city streets. Jewelry, buttons, belts, and shoe buckles all had a luminous glow. Lilly Daché's collection of January 1942 featured luminous fabric gloves and a Scotch cap ornamented with a round crystal reflector, similar to those found on bicycles. In May 1943, the Brooklyn Museum displayed millinery with a practical, not pretty, orientation: women defense worker hats.

Meanwhile, in Paris, fashion responded to the Occupation with bravado. Although 70 French couturiers were still allowed to produce during wartime, a radical and aggressive style originated on the streets. Exaggerated and frivolous, ungainly and awkward— clothing, shoes, and millinery took on an ad-libbed quality, shaped by shortages of nearly every material, dye, and especially heating fuel.

By 1942, Parisian fashion invented a theory of sabotage: the more material the French used, the less would be available for the Germans. Skirts be-

Characteristic of the late 1940s is a simple hat with a one-note ornament, OPPOSITE. A varation on the theme, the hat, BELOW, has shoulder-tickling feathers (label: Don Marshall).

came wider and shorter, jackets flared and longer, chapeaux became gigantic and cushion-shaped. Obviously home-made, these hats were pieced together, quilt style, from recycled fabric. The Frenchwoman's ingenuity was boundless: Brie and Camembert cheese boxes were recycled into headwear, string crocheted into snoods, and socks transformed into snug toppers. Agnès, one of the milliners still at work, laboriously fashioned strips of wood shavings into a sailor hat. Even city parks became a supply source, as women gathered wild bird feathers.

The nose-thumbing, anti-German attitude of this absurdist headgear was finally recognized. In mid-May of 1943, "fantastically voluminous" headwear was forbidden by German government decree.

Nevertheless, exaggeration continued: skirts and sleeves ballooned; bulky orthopediclike shoes and clogs teetered on platforms of cork or wood.

A little over six months after the Occupation was over, the picture hadn't changed. *Life* gave one of the first glimpses of postwar Paris in the fall of 1944. It was not a comforting vision: "The clothing is arrogant, often mannish." Coiffures as well as hats were still high: fabric turbans topped with feathers towered nearly a foot tall, or resembled such objects as "balloons, minarets, chef's caps."

The desperate, extravagant millinery of wartime was never equaled. Slowly, once peace was declared, fashion assumed a sober style. In the fall of 1944, six months after the truce in

Europe, Parisians wore sedate black tulle hairnets, ornamented with a Cross of Lorraine, or a cross emblazoned with the name of a city (New York, Paris, Los Angeles). As a penalty for using too much fabric for his hats, Balenciaga was forbidden to produce millinery. He offered a millinery substitution in the spring of 1944: hair worn in a thick coil atop the head. (The style was created for Balenciaga by his associate, Guillaume d'Attainville.)

view: "Hats after V-J day must be optimistic, home-coming hats to greet the boys. They must be exciting, new, free from foreign influence. They must be American born and bred." Variety

Although the hatless movement gathered steam, ladies who lunched were always suitably hatted, **BELOW**. Giddy toppers in Easter colors would have been perfect for teatime in spring, **OPPOSITE**.

worn day and night—were cupped tightly over the face and under the chin, like a feedbag. For the first time in years, hats sat properly on the head, minus the elastic straps and hatpins that had secured them at their formerly crazy angles.

Contrast was another theme. Wide-scale platter hats balanced toothpick-thin dresses and hip-draped or peplumed dinner suits. A velvet chapeau of vermilion roses or a wide hat of

Between the end of the war and the debut of Christian Dior's New Look, American fashion followed an understated, feminine style that had a real purpose. The milliner Walter Florell spelled it out in *Millinery Trade Re-*

Viewed from back and front, an oversize beret—a trefoil of bugle beads—sports the fancy handwork characteristic of the 1940s, **PAGES 66–67**.

and femininity were the bywords. There were circles of ostrich, marabou powderpuffs, platters and ballerina wreaths of foliage, fruit, and flowers, straw beehives, pillboxes, and the masculine derby fronted with a veil. Templets, half-bonnets, calots, cloches, and neat little skullcaps worked with the new, shorter hairstyles. The helmet/snood with ties that wrapped around the head and neck was still in the vocabulary. Veils—

draped bronze satin complemented a severe black street suit; a pouff of satin, bows, or flowers, a houndstooth suit; a shiny satin blouse, a menswear tweed suit. Sequin trim was not unusual for a hat worn at nine A.M.

Couture designs began to trickle back into America in the spring of 1945. Still reminiscent of wartime Paris, millinery had an uneasy, jarring character that was strangely glamorous, as in a white velvet topper like a

giddy chef's hat, banded with mink. International and ethnic styles, a dominant influence in the 1930s, subsided during the war, when several countries turned up on the wrong side of the battle lines. When the turban—high and draped—came back in the fall of 1944, it signaled a readiness for exaggeration once again.

The most notable example of exaggeration was the New Look of 1947. Although the long-skirted, round shouldered, pulled-in waist look had been part of fashion's dance before the war, it was Christian Dior who finally partnered it to the runway. Unabashed luxury made a rebound. As Dior stated, "In an epoch as somber as ours, one must fight for luxury inch by inch." Dior's claim was fulfilled by sweeping skirts of 10 to 25 yards of fabric, the perfect ensemble of hat, high-heeled pumps, gloves, umbrella, and pearls.

To balance the big skirt, the hat hugged the head. *Vogue* described Dior's signature accessory for fall 1947 as "half-hair, half-hat": a flat toque garnished with just a filter of veiling or a spiky aigrette plume, and worn cocked to one side of the head. The New Look silhouette was also balanced by the flip side of the small hat: the wide horizontal of a velvet platter.

Dior's side-tilted hat was prophetic. Taken up in 1948, the asymmetrical line was practically a cause célèbre through the rest of the decade. Collections featured handkerchief hems, one-shouldered dresses, and side-buttoned bodices; Charles James created masterfully uneven draped jackets. Even shoes had asymmetrical straps.

The New Look chapeau, such as the "mermaid" cap, **ABOVE**, hugged the head. A wide-at-the-sides hat also accompanied the New Look, the style that closed the decade, **OPPOSITE**.

Hats swelled from high to low at the sides, jutted forward, sported off-center pleats, creases, and draping. *Vogue* remarked that the lopsided chapeau "does almost anything except balance evenly on your head like a good-little-girl's hat." Accentuating the off-balance sensation, the crown merged into the brim in a smooth, unbroken line. Though her influence was waning, even Elsa Schiaparelli followed fashion's herd. Her fall 1948 collection starred a tilted toque, a tipped tricorne of feathers, and a calfskin bicorne canted over one eye.

Dior's asymmetrical "broken egg" hat, introduced in 1948, showed a playfulness recently absent from millinery. His egg hat was skullcap snug,

and broken into jagged points over the forehead. His other hats had the same peculiar style: a leopard skullcap sprouted curved devil horns on the side. There were panther pixie hats, helmets, and casquettes with claws, beaks, and puffy bird shapes, made up in velvet, velour, fur, and embroidered fabric.

Finally, hats made their ultimate joke, mimicking hairstyles: the gamine cut, duplicated in colored feathers, was a mainstay in the millinery vocabulary until well into the 1950s.

The little hat—so light a woman could forget it was there—finally reached a not-unexpected dénouement: hatlessness. The chapeau began to slip from its position as the mark of a lady. Those who went without included the young co-ed set (the dilettante debutantes had lost their trendsetting power). In warm weather, a clutch of flowers fastened to a hair clip could now be called a "hat." Millinery sources referred to the summer of 1940 as the "siege of hatlessness." In 1947, another crisis struck: coats were made with hoods. By 1949, hatlessness was so rampant that Mr. Fred of John-Frederics forced all visitors to wear hats. Outside the showroom, his majordomo, dressed in a Revolutionary costume of powdered wig and tricorne, chanted, "Everybody must wear a hat. You look smarter in a hat. The time of hatlessness is over." *Millinery Monitor* reported in 1949 that Mr. Fred was obeyed by "even those recalcitrant members of the fashion press who, according to their own statements, 'hate hats.' " Mr. Fred's ploy was just a finger in the dike against hatlessness.

the
50s

white gloves on the steering wheel

The sophisticated woman of the 1950s cast a strange shadow: string-bean skinny neck and legs projecting from a dress shaped like a spindle, balloon, barrel, umbrella, or pyramid. Atop her head sat a hat shaped like a cartwheel, a meringue, a bell, a champagne cork, a pie plate, or an upside-down mixing bowl. Bad posture completed the 1950s look: shoulders hunched, pelvis tipped. Accessories added to the discomfort: high-rising on stiletto

The last year has been one of the most confusing in fashion history. Women are bemused, baffled, and bewildered. Freshly coined fashion terms gabble for attention in their brains—chemise, trapeze, blouson, baby doll, Empire line.

—*THE NEW YORK TIMES*

pointed heels, an irritatingly geometric handbag over the arm.

The fashion plate's casual counterpart cast a different kind of shadow: wearing slim toreador trousers, a turtleneck, and flat slippers, she pulled her hair back into a tight ponytail, and never wore a hat. Both styles shared the same approach to beauty. A mouth paled with frosted lipstick. Eyebrows arched artificially over the "gazelle eye," drawn with brushstrokes of black or shiny white eye liner over fake lashes, and a foundation of technicolor shadow (blue or turquoise).

Stark clothing begged for accessories; flash and jingle made an elaborate counterpoint. Costume jewelry was absolutely de rigueur and jumbo-sized: bib necklaces and chokers, arm-loads of bangle and charm bracelets, chandelier earrings, and golf ball—sized rings. "Done up like a Christmas tree" was a compliment. Other acccessory desirables were anything mink—preferably in one of the new mutant pale colors—or crocodile.

The accessories of social life were likewise exaggerated, and somewhat

The straw toque topped with wiggy curls, **PAGE 72**, represents the stark, often witty, aerospace look of 1950s millinery. Other examples of oddball streamlining are the woven straw pillbox, **BELOW**, and the velvet beanie shaped like a cartoon flower, **OPPOSITE ABOVE**. Mamie Eisenhower's wardrobe also amused on occasion, **OPPOSITE BELOW**.

on the nervous side: filter cigarettes, bone-dry martinis, and tiny purse- or vest pocket-sized pillboxes, loaded with tranquilizers or "uppers."

The Korean War was just one source of anxiety for the grey-flannel-suit types. On the home front, teenagers gathered their forces, and by mid-decade, they were armed with 50 percent more spending money than their prewar counterparts. They had their own dress code, and antiestablishment hero types, from Elvis Presley to the Beats. Fashion was prepared to meet them on their own ground: "junior" clothes appeared, and in London, Mary Quant opened her Bazaar boutique, which sold short and radical clothing.

Between these extremes was the

ladylike First Lady, Mamie Eisen-hower. Mamie's sensible to dull ward-robe featured full skirts, dangling bracelets, and Peter Pan collars, set off by her trademark Buster Brown bangs. No client of the couturiers, she ordered her clothes by phone from newspaper advertisements. Mamie's down-home, all-American image struck a chord with 1950s women. As a housewife told *The New York Times* in 1960, "I've always sympathized with her, because I've never been able to do anything with my hair, either."

The lineup of glamorous fashion in-fluences included the frosty Princess Grace (Monaco), Princess Margaret

(England), and America's princess Babe Paley (American-born and best-dressed). Show business stylemongers were a varied bunch: Elizabeth Taylor and Audrey Hepburn, Brigitte Bardot and Doris Day, *My Fair Lady, The King and I,* and *To Catch a Thief.*

Even cars had the same diversity: the station wagon and the Thunderbird were driveway companions. Life on four wheels centered around the sub-urbs, where the postwar generation settled in droves. Casual, at-home en-tertaining accompanied this nesting

instinct. The patio and the barbeque grill took center stage in the acres of greenery. *Flair* magazine summed up the 1950s lifestyle as "evenings of canasta, conversation and dinner-built-around-a-casserole—when a billowing skirt would be plainly off key."

In the kitchen, a woman could boil dinner in a plastic bag in 14 minutes, and heat the rest of the meal in a pan made from the same material used for rocket-nose cones. Nevertheless, she obeyed the rules. Wrist-length and immaculate white gloves remained a caste sign. Even though *Sputnik* soared overhead, a lady still needed something to cover hers. An etiquette book chided, "A lady never runs, goes out of the house without a hat, puts her gloves on as she leaves the house or wears red." Running was out of the question, but color came on strong. By the end of the decade, hot pink and orange was an acceptable scheme.

Led by couturiers Dior, Balmain, Balenciaga, Fath, and Desses, clothing of the 1950s changed dramatically from season to season. The silhouette varied from Dior's wide-as-a-house coats to mermaid skirts with jutting lines to Balenciaga's jacket with hourglass sleeves. The chapeau with a distinct, clean line was a foil for these dramatics. Nominating Balenciaga's Chinese red beret as *the* hat for fall 1950, *Vogue* gushed, "We think you will see this draped, plump, cushiony beret, or its immediate descendants, dotted all over America this autumn like bright little exclamation points." The most popular millinery for the early 1950s was the mushroom, with a neat brim and a shape that was clean

Early 1950s hats kept to the tight silhouette stylish in the late 1940s, **ABOVE**. By decade's end, hats were stripped down to a wisp of veiling—so minimal there was no room to fit even the milliner's label, **OPPOSITE**.

and simple, but just the tiniest bit puffy.

Fashion was fixed on "big" textured fabric. In the vocabulary: teddy bear cloth, rough-as-a-doormat fleeces, and shaggy/knobby wools. "I adore you, but you dress women like armchairs," was Coco Chanel's backhanded compliment to Dior, whose 1950 collection featured upholstery-thick wool coats. Splendidly textured in furry brushed felt, hatter's plush, velour, and spun nylon, hats got rough, too. A 1951 mix-of-textures pointer from milliner Lilly Daché in *Hats:* "Pair a smooth, sleek hat with a coat or dress of shaggy, deep-pile material, and vice versa." For summer 1951, Jacques

Heim created oddball combinations, such as tambourines and pillboxes of wood chips, willow, wheat, and barley; a cloche crowned with cork; and a straw beret with a visor of tree bark.

Hats were resplendent with the

trimming that the severe clothing lacked. Feathers continued to preen in the spotlight, even after the New York State Conservation Department ruled that wild bird plumage was outlawed as of April 15, 1950. (Three tons of confiscated feathers were consigned to the bonfire.) Tiny mirrors, ball fringe, passementerie, braid, paillettes, glass jet, rhinestones, beads, and pearls took their place. Dior's signature oval rhinestone mound brooches were fastened at cuffs, hips, and chapeau ear flaps. A sapphire velvet beret might be matched with a shoulder scarf, both strewn with cabochon jewels.

Veils—in color as well as metallics —were part of the display, and one fashion writer even recommended matching veil to eye shadow color. Juliet caps and turbans were put together entirely of veiling.

The chapeau palette included ebullient colors such as orange, red, and green, plus the standard black. Like the texture play of the fabric, contrast was key to a new look for accessories,

too. One "don't" from Bettina Ballard of *Vogue* was a color-matched hat, bag, gloves, and shoes.

While color was used with a bold new freedom, Christian Dior had a stranglehold on style. In the 1950s, he accounted for a whopping 66 percent of the total French couture exports. Coco Chanel delivered the knockout punch to his shackling fashions: embracing a woman in his dresses, she claimed, was like "grasping a birdcage."

Engineering a comeback at the age of 71, Chanel put women at ease in

comfortable and relatively unconstructed cardigan suits. "I want mannequins with bosoms and hips. Today's look is the elegance of the cemetery; these women are ghosts," Chanel crowed in the February 1954 *Vogue*. The flimsy, precariously perched little hats that accompanied cemetery elegance were not for her. For her first collection, the Chanel mannequins wore little-girl bows at the back of their heads, or sailor hats.

Other milliners were less direct than Chanel, borrowing bits and pieces from a smattering of sources: approxima-

Flowers were a signature that also lasted throughout the decade. Associated with England and the coronation of Queen Elizabeth II in 1954, they were scattered on hats, and served as a motif for everything from costume jewelry to print fabrics. In a switch from their usual season, flowered hats were paired with wintertime fur coats.

By the fall of 1955, the "hattier" hat was hailed, and it was high, big, and bulky. The wedding of Grace Kelly and the play *My Fair Lady,* with its 'teens-era costumes by Cecil Beaton, also gave more elaborate headgear a shot in the arm. Big hats worked as a counterbalance to the freshest silhouette from Paris: wider shoulders. There was a coolie sailor, a flying saucer, a platter, a deep casserole dish. Milliner Adolfo—just getting attention as a designer at Emme—produced an overgrown newsboy cap of leopard. More extreme shapes included a droopy mushroom, a deflated soufflé, a

tions of samurai helmets, pagodas, rippling Charlottes, draped hoods, bumpers, capelines, baby bonnets, and chignon caps. New terms were coined to fit these hat hybrids: the bicorne-bonnet, tricorne-cloche, sailor-coolie, helmet-toque. The cloche, reintroduced by Christian Dior late in 1953, became a fixture of every season through the rest of the decade.

These face-framing styles were a perfect foil for the beauty ideal of the day: dark, emphatic, painted-on eyebrows and a new short, tousled, nibbled-looking haircut, called the "Italian" coiff. It accompanied the boom in casual dress—Italian and

American sportswear. Paris stuck to luxury and fine tailoring.

Fur continued fashion's preoccupation with texture. Hats made of the stuff were big-scale, squashy, mushy, awkward-looking platters of beaver, mink, astrakhan, or shaggy velours and angoras. Some of them were shoulder-wide, a horizontal punctuation to the long, lean, Ichabod Crane silhouette of clothing. Balenciaga introduced a powderpuff version: a towering busby-like pouff of white fox or blue swansdown, centered with a giant silk rose. American milliner Walter Florell's remarkable creation: a picture hat and wrap stole, both of pale pink beaver.

squeezed-in-the-center spool cloche, and shakos. The French contributed a new hat shape and title to millinery. *"Bourrelets"* were "bumper" chapeaux.

Bulk without weight was the milliner's task. Rough materials (straw) and airy or smooth fabrics (organdy and silk) were perfect for this large but lightweight direction. Fabrics were made to look bulkier via shirring, stitching, and gathering. Rose Sapphire used 50 layers of tulle in three different shades of green to create a weightlessly sizeable chapeau. William J's massive bomb of yellow plumage came in a heroic haystack size. Emme's 1956 offering was also a hard-to-miss triumph: deep as a small laundry basket, it was shoulder-wide, with a polka dot scarf around the crown.

Headwear picked up on the intense, contrasting colors used by other accessories. Olive, sapphire, turquoise, and teal blues were popular—alone or

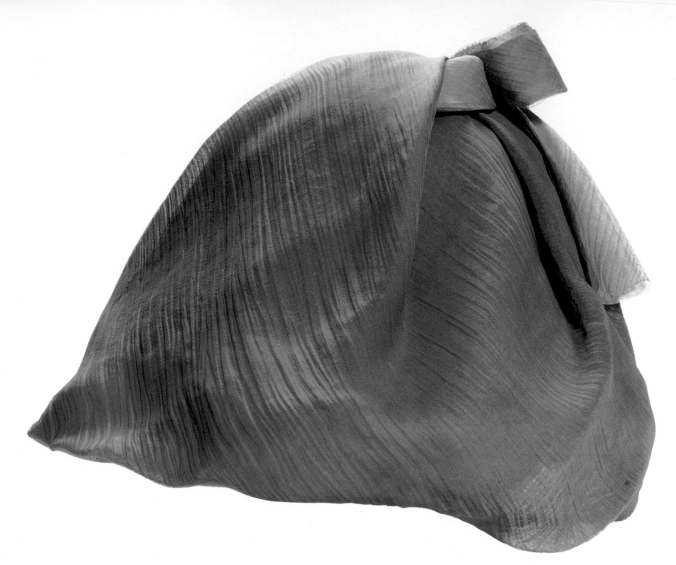

mixed together—for the chunky, multistrand bead necklaces.

Straw and raffia éntered the millinery scene in a less sedate guise, too. In 1956, anticipating Hawaii's statehood in 1959, hats took a tropical turn. Even if leisure time in the tropics wasn't possible, fun hattery made it look that way. Suitable for town wear, the backyard, and the beach, these generously scaled toppers carried a load of goofy decorations. A "boozing bonnet" sported bottle caps, a champagne cork, and a jeweled bottle opener. Straw hand and beach bags were often made to match.

Milliners also took a creative ap-

A cloche turns into a beehive hat (label: Bergdorf Goodman), **ABOVE**. Extreme "fun" hats took to the sun, **OPPOSITE ABOVE**. The Empire dress style of 1958 sparked similar waisted silhouettes in millinery, such as the silk hat (label: Lilly Daché), **OPPOSITE BELOW**.

proach to a growing aesthetic problem: covering up curlers or a less-than-perfect hairdo. Their solutions were terrycloth or linen kerchiefs, bonnets, and cloches equipped with fake hair bangs in the front.

The New York Times hailed these innovative styles as the millinery industry's "Joan of Arc." For the first time

in years, hats had a radical new look that made all other hats obsolete. In 1956 sales were sparked (8 to 10 percent) for the first time in years. The year 1957 had a promising start, buoyed by the sales increase of 1956. As a business booster, fashion authorities struggled to establish a difference between the 1956 and the 1957 hat crop. *Hats* noted that "freak" millinery was almost completely absent from 1957 styles. *Harper's Bazaar* observed that "men are going to have to stop laughing at women's hats this spring" since "the day of the hard, smart shocker hat is past." Despite their good intentions, headwear in 1957

looked only fractionally different; women shrugged and bought 31 percent fewer hats. It was a nasty blow.

Seeking a scapegoat for the unchanging and monotonous hat styles, milliners fingered Paris couturiers. A new silhouette was introduced every season, but it didn't create a radically new hat. Premiering late in 1957, the chemise or "sack" dress hung straight from the shoulders and narrowed toward the hem. Dior got the credit—and the blame—for its creation. Roundly denounced by men, the sack dress also went by the less kindly monikers the nightshirt, the limp look, and the shoplifter's delight. The sack had one plus: it was short enough to show off legs clad in the new crazily colored stockings. Despite its unkind reception, the sack was a smash, the best sellers in the spring 1958 *Sears, Roebuck Catalogue.*

Twenty-one-year-old Yves Saint Laurent launched another shape—the trapeze—with his first collection for Dior, early in 1958. The trapeze was a plain, tailored pyramid, with small shoulders and a wide skirt. The Empire line followed in the fall of 1958: dresses were sashed, tied, and even belted under the bosom.

collections in Paris and New York, and created lace cloches, frilly eyelet nightcaps, and puffy Charlottes, linked to the Napoleonic motif of the Empire line. Empire also inspired cloches and bubble-turbans, cinched at their mid-section with a narrow leather belt, buckle, or bow.

Printed fabrics were important in 1958: everything from loud florals to dot-decorated glazed chintz, silk, chiffons, and cotton. Even strawcloth was printed in a pattern. Printed wool jersey, used for hats and dresses, was accepted as correct wear year 'round. In summertime, face-shading, droopy-brimmed fabric cloches were matched to dresses, such as a black-and-white striped cotton and a rose print silk.

For all these silhouettes—the chemise/sack, trapeze, and Empire—millinery was nearly interchangeable. For example, the cloche, the wig-toque, and the bubble-turban were held over from 1957 to 1958. The sole innovation for 1957 was Dior's back-dipped sou'wester, which accompanied his low-backed spring dresses.

Beginning in 1957, the fabric hat was the new millinery star—draped, lightweight, but voluminous—a soft contrast to exact tailoring. Fabric was also draped over hat brims or crowns or stitched over a body of another material, such as straw or felt. Milliners took note of the avalanches of organza and chiffon that drifted through the

Velour and felt were treated as if they were fabric, puffed up into beehives and bubbles, then crushed, dented, ridged, and twisted into shape. Fabrics that had bulk without weight—especially mohair—were the most popular fabrics in 1958.

"Wig-toques," as they were tagged by milliners, were close-fitting hats of feathers, fur, flowers, or manipulated fabrics that completely covered the head. Pierre Cardin's spring 1958 collection featured slightly comic bubble-shaped wig-toquery, which echoed his "puffball"-shaped skirts in the same collection. Parisian milliner Claude St. Cyr's spring 1959 wig-toque was of uncurled ostrich, shaded and shaped to look exactly like a smooth bouffant head of hair, and trimmed with a hair bow in front. Other wig-toques were of plumage laid perfectly flat, creating an effect something like a pixie hairdo.

Alarm bells should have gone off when the venerable Lilly Daché put her hats in second place: she opened a beauty salon in New York, signing up hair stylist Kenneth. Over the next few

The "wig-toque" vocabulary included a "Harpo Marx" version in silk curls, **ABOVE LEFT**, and an untamed chapeau of coq feathers on a velvet crown, **BELOW LEFT** (labels, both hats: William J.). The sculpted silhouette called for equally severe hattery. Neat little hats that sat properly on the head still had a slightly jarring quality (label: Sally Victor), **OPPOSITE**.

years, wigs, clips, veiling novelties, head warmers, and hairpieces would assume some of the importance of millinery. Even swim caps took on a new

chic: Adolfo's models for the U.S. Rubber Company were made of a waterproof material that looked like velvet. Unfortunately, the hat industry failed to recognize these accessories as profitable sidelines, and so most of the marginal hattery was made by non-milliners, even though it was sold in store millinery departments.

The theatricality that simmered throughout the 1950s came to a rolling boil in 1959. Skirts skimmed the knee. Coats appeared to be cut from entire bolts of fabric. Soap-bubble—sized pearls adorned ears and massive jet and crystal chokers ringed necks. Shoes were pointed and ornamented.

And hats? Millinery "brain fatigue" was the term tossed around by a fashion magazine. Aside from a few stylistic differences, hats could boast no major silhouette changes from the previous year. Despite new textures and materials and a few new shapes—a tall, rounded bullet imported from France, for example, called *obus,* that transformed women into coneheads—millinery headed into a commercial and creative nosedive.

Some conservatives held their ground. Etiquette maven Emily Post still advised, as late as 1957, "Notwithstanding the continued practice of going bareheaded, best taste exacts that a hat be worn with street clothes in all cities whether day time or night." In spite of Post and the other hard-liners, the hat-wearing code was under review. Confusion developed about what was truly proper attire. A reader questioned *The Cleveland Plain Dealer* in 1955: as the only woman hatted at a recent dinner party, was she inappro-

priately dressed? The newspaper's fashion adviser reassured:

> Just because the other women in the dining room were casually and incorrectly dressed doesn't mean they were right. The effect of too casual dressing, regardless of

ager's perception of Who Wears a Hat. According to *Hats,* the new generation believed hats were supported by two female types—successful women and married women. Both groups had a faintly old-fashioned aura. Some mem-

when I go shopping. I get better service.'' In the slang du jour, the cookie was crumbling.

Though hats sales slumped throughout the period, the 1950s stands as the millinery twilight, the

time or place, has gone too far. Some women, like teenagers, follow mass fads and customs, believing that, ''If Mrs. Jones does it, so can I.''

For a time, headgear proceeded according to normal. ''Executive'' working women continued to wear hats even in the office, as opposed to the lowly file clerks who went hatless and displayed nonexecutive behavior: at their desks they would ''comb out their bobby pins from 9:00 to 9:30 every morning,'' claimed *Hats* in 1950.

Those examples jibed with the teen-

A constructed turban of silk satin, made in 1955 (label: Mme. Udes), mimics sculpted hairdos, OPPOSITE. A constructed silk faille cocktail hat pays homage to a bull fighter's headdress and queue—and its creator's Spanish heritage (label: Balenciaga), ABOVE LEFT. Another master couturier topped Audrey Hepburn with a pointed woven chapeau, ABOVE RIGHT.

bers of the younger set—both women and men—had never owned a hat, for various reasons. *Mademoiselle* staffers gave the reason, ''A hat makes me look older'' and the positive ''I wear a hat

last great decade of hat wearing as it had been practiced. Desperate milliners created a hit list of contributors to the hat's decline. They included the press, wigmakers, Paris couturiers, American milliners, men, women, the uncooperative teenagers, store buyers, and the stores themselves.

The single object that contributed to the hat's decline wasn't found on the milliner's list: the rattail comb. A hat had nowhere to perch atop the ratted bouffant hairstyles. Real hair came to be handled as if it were faux: it was curled, folded, and pouffed into draped, semibouffant arrangements, or combed and sprayed into a haystack, a hive, or a "dramatically careless coiff." Hairstyles were also supplemented with fake hair "switches." These fantastical shapes were made possible by hairspray, and sales of that new and high-profile beauty aid increased 280 percent from 1954 to 1957. Groused *The New York Times* in 1958, "Women look as if they had combed their tresses with a Mixmaster."

The only millinery that could be worn without flattening the heaped, high-rising dos were the bandeau-coiffs or whimsies of the late 1950s, which appeared to have been created following the maxim "Less is more." This millinery was little more than a headband or flimsy wire construction, sprouting an umbrella of stiffened veiling, ribbons, feathers, flowers. Some "whimsies" were a spritz of veiling stuck with a bow, which arched weightlessly over the head. Worn day or night, whimsies accounted for

slightly less than 25 percent of the wholesale millinery business in 1959.

The cousins of the whimsies were the wig-toques, which still enjoyed a run of popularity. These exquisite, slightly campy hats were composed of materials that covered the entire head: little "curls" or pleats of veiling or tuille, and flowers. "What could be more flattering, more feminine or elegant than these ravishing perukes of shirred or ruched veilings, these draped bubble-turbans, these puffy

berets and bonnets of embroidered tulle . . . ?" was the dreamy question from a 1959 issue of *Hats*.

Although *Vogue* scolded in 1959, "Who doesn't wear a hat, right now, is the woman who's deliberately bent on passing up one of the greatest outbreaks of fashion enchantment to come out of Paris in years," apparently most women were exactly that willful. Although millinery sales had crawled up 2 percent in 1959, this closed a decade in which sales plummeted.

By decade's end, the hat was merely a token, riding on the masterpiece of the coiffeur's art. Clare Boothe Luce dated herself as a lady from an earlier era when she closed a TV interview in 1958 with the old-fashioned exit line, "Excuse me. I am going to get myself a new hat."

An all-over design of beads snaked across a hat from the early 1950s, LEFT; roughly woven straw circles a picture hat, TOP; and pheasant feathers swirl around a toque, ABOVE. Feathers cover an all-season helmet (label: Christian Dior—New York), OPPOSITE.

the 60s

what's happenin'?

Ever poetic, *Vogue* editor Diana Vreeland rhapsodized about the 1960s beauty: she had "jeune fille" breasts and "knees like little peaches." Legs were as "smooth as a pair of flying silk ribbons, as unmarred by time as the legs of a ten-year-old girl." *Women's Wear Daily* bypassed the flying metaphor, instead labeling the 1960s ideal "a locomotive."

Stick-thin models powered the fashion magazines: Twiggy, Veruschka, Penelope Tree, Jean Shrimpton.

The mood of Paris is savage and fun —old lady-like elegance has had it.

—WOMEN'S WEAR DAILY

In Paris, couturier Castillo put even more juvenile *jeune fille* goddesses on the runway: modeling his collection were 15-year-old girls. *Seventeen* magazine observed that the stylish female "weighs more with her makeup on." "What has size to do with beauty now?" demanded *Vogue* in 1963. "Only everything. . . . The eye is bigger, deeper, pitched into exaggerated shadow, rimmed with a thickened fringe of eyelashes. The mouth is stronger, glossed for heightened fullness." Quirky was favored over classical; even singer Barbra Streisand's kooky individuality got rave reviews.

Sculptural shapes ruled the decade, such as the cotton bubble, **PAGE 92.** Early 1960s millinery clung to styles set in the 1950s, as with the straw beehive (bird added; label: Don Anderson), **OPPOSITE.** By 1967, hats had become mere lampshades: a calfskin version (label: Nina Ricci), **ABOVE LEFT.** Another bubble shows an Eastern influence, (label: Adolfo), **BELOW LEFT.**

Fashion was every bit the match for the bold 1960s beauty. Style changed, rapid-fire, throughout the decade. Quoted in *Life* in 1965, feminist Gloria Steinem ran through the catalogue of 1960s choices: "a well-groomed 12-year-old, a motorcycle cop, a Botticelli heroine or Jean Harlow." Steinem could have supplemented that list with two more looks: space queen and earth mother. Taking a brief spell in the lights were designers and studios from Paco Rabanne's plastic disc tunics to the Biba boutique's droopy satin dresses to the severe tailored geometry of Courrèges.

Keeping up with that dizzy succession was expensive. During the youth reign, from 1963 to 1967, *Fortune* magazine reported that the money spent on clothing rose 40 percent. Meanwhile, the number of teenagers went up 24 percent, as the rest of the total population increased only 8 percent. Although the word "youthquake" hadn't been coined by 1960, *Vogue* had already acknowledged that youth called all the fashion shots.

The old school had its representatives, such as the New Frontier wife of the Kennedy era, who still followed the rules of the coordinated costume. The signature elements of the Jackie Kennedy style included plain "little nothing" dresses in sherbet colors, white gloves, low-heeled shoes, a small, boxy bag. Jackie's example also converted millions of women over to a smooth bouffant hairdo: hers was tapemeasured at 24 inches in circumference. It became part of the vocabulary of every American beauty salon.

Hats—notably Jackie's signature pillbox—figured in the fashion picture, but they were included as a token, rather than an accessory worthy of individual attention. Hatlessness wasn't quite the same rebellion in the 1960s as it had been in the 1950s. The fight had already grown so cold that wearing a hat projected a faintly antiestablishment, nonconformist attitude. Even the way they were sold changed in the 1960s. Older women and conservatives who still clung to the millinery habit indulged it in department stores, where they were presented with a rehash of styles from the 1950s. The "in" younger crowd shopped the flour-

From a millinery perspective, the 1960s had two sides: the ebullient flower-power wig hat, **OPPOSITE**, a holdover from the 1950s, and the stark, structured pillbox that Jackie Kennedy made her trademark during the White House years, **ABOVE**.

ishing boutiques, which had recently come of age. Hats available in boutiques were frequently one-of-a-kind, or made by small-time designers. The crafting of these hats—the overstitched suede floppies, the grommeted berets and the Beatles caps—required no traditional millinery skills, or even a traditional milliner.

A few milliners saw the writing on the wall. To survive, it wasn't enough

to market a cheap line of hats; several of the "name" milliners—Adolfo, Halston, Emme, Mr. John—branched out into clothing. It was a sign of the times when milliner William J presented a price reduction along with his spring collection. He would now do only one fitting per hat, he explained—a switch from the five or six his private clients were accustomed to—charging a maximum of $59 a hat.

Hair continued to defeat the hat at every turn. As much time and often money went into hair maintenance as clothing; a woman might spend $8 of her $75-a-week salary on hair care. Master coiffeur Vidal Sassoon commanded $25 for a cut. Elaborate arrangements also made hair more

interesting than hats: the coiffeur Kenneth was praised for cramming 12 hairpieces into a single do for a photo session. The fake hair industry boomed: in 1966, an estimated 30 million hairpieces were sold in the United States. At home, hair was set with Scotch tape, rolled around orange juice cans, or even straightened with an iron.

Answering the challenge, milliners made hats that looked like wigs—a simple solution to a complex and no-win situation. Why, even being called best dressed in the 1960s was hardly standard stuff. In 1965, *Women's Wear Daily* described the era's stylish fun couple: ''There is Sonny who doesn't own a tie and Cher who doesn't own a dress.'' It's a sure thing hats weren't part of Cher's wardrobe, either.

At the beginning of the decade the

Streamlined, smooth, unadorned helmets were nicknamed ''cosmonaut casques'' after the Soviet space venture. The angular helmet, **ABOVE**, is reminiscent of the late 1920s. The asymmetrical satin casque (label: Nina Ricci), **OPPOSITE ABOVE**, and sketch (by Marie Christiane), **OPPOSITE BELOW**, share the same angular profile.

hotshots of couture—Saint Laurent, Dior, Cardin, Laroche, Ricci, Given-

Fur hats were seen as the perfect frame for the new face of beauty: dark-rimmed eyes, pale pink lips. In 1960 there were monstrous, enormous busbys. Dior introduced fur-spiraled cones, and put a pompon-topped fur watch cap with a tweed suit.

Cardin showed Davy Crockett caps in 1961, and newcomer Courrèges created a startling first collection: a dark green tweed suit with a bright pink

beaver hat. Fur even made a show around the throat, as the 1960s collars were replaced by "necklace" scarves of fur. The perfect combination was a sable hat with a small sable collar.

Dior was the knit cap's patron. His surprise was a rib knit cap, "like a little Vermont boy's winter headgear—only more mondaine." What was surprising was the way the cap was shown: not with a casual sports outfit, but a so-

chy, and Lanvin-Castill—still held on to the acrobatics of fine tailoring. The line in 1960 was knee-length skirts, fitted to the body, with a slightly dropped waist. The suit—tweeds woven in stirring colors—remained the warhorse in women's closets. There were signs that fashion was loosening up: it was noted that Saint Laurent removed all inner construction from his clothes, and used black—"the Beat's own color"—in his color schemes. There were strange juxtapositions, such as the bells sewn under the hems of Ricci's cocktail dresses, knitted pompons instead of buttons, culotte skirts.

Accessories possessed the same kind of offhand, daring attitude in the collections. Shoes had flat, spatula-shaped toes instead of spike points. Necklaces were weighed down by hefty pendants. Millinery was gripped by two styles—the fur hat and the knit cap—that shook up the conventional notion of what made a suitable fashion match.

phisticated dress with a matching, set-in turtleneck. The ensemble was titled "Café de Flore" after the student's and intellectual's hangout.

Chanel stuck to a more conventional formula: hats in the same multicolored tweed as her suits. They were worn tilted over the eyes, garnished with a long-tailed bow that trailed down over the neck. The same formula of tweed hat matched with jacket or coat was recycled in 1961, with fringe and a scarf added to the ensemble. Milliner Tatiana of Saks Fifth Avenue gave her customers the same scenario for evening. Her rich, metal-shot brocade dinner dresses and jackets had a draped turban in the same material.

Thanks to summertime lightweight materials, hats grew to a shape that was "between an egg and an inflated balloon," as *Hats* phrased it. Dior favored this extremism: his tall, undecorated helmets were elegant in paillasson, piqué, and later, even in leather. (The lower-priced Miss Dior hat line was launched in New York in 1960.) Givenchy did a square cloche in white strawcloth that looked like a four-sided Japanese lantern.

A wild headdress of straw (label: Pucci), **ABOVE LEFT**; a free fall of blossoms (label: Don Marshall), **ABOVE RIGHT**; and a net hood swarming with blossoms (label: Guy Laroche), **OPPOSITE BELOW**, are intended to frame the face. Meanwhile, as ever-more outré headgear expressed the desperation of the collapsing industry, Chanel stuck to the classics, matching her millinery to her suits, such as the wool tweed skimmer, **OPPOSITE ABOVE**.

Straw was used in quantity, along with organdy, silk, and tulle, sometimes stitched and shirred together into cabbagelike multiple layers and mixes of multiple colors. Both New York and Paris favored patching contrasting fabrics and colors together, such as mink with satin, straw with ribbon, or four assorted shades of violet velvet.

The cloche and turban were the silhouettes for summer and winter. Wide or narrow-brimmed, the cloche was featured in everything from pigeon and hackle feathers to gold kid and leopard. At its most ordinary in felt, the cloche resembled a man's hat. The turban was the expression of exotica. In comparison to fashion's newly developing clean, modern lines, the Far Eastern-style dazzle of this fabric

seemed dated. Nevertheless, velvet, brocade, tulle, and lamé were wound into domes and minaret silhouettes; printed challis and jersey were the materials for the same style, interpreted for daytime wear.

The freshest headwear silhouette to come out of Paris in the fall of 1961 was a disaster for the bouffant hairdo: Dior's hood was shown with a black velvet dinner suit—plain or jet pailletted all over—worn over a beanie.

The passion for shaggy fabric that ruled the 1950s was translated into pattern in the 1960s. Svend, who designed for Jacques Heim, launched tall toques of novelty straws in two and three colors, woven into large and small checks, stripes, and plaids. It was a perfect match for the gingham that turned up in springtime, as brown-and-white checks were found on everything from bathing suits to evening dresses. The same fabric even covered back-of-the-head pillboxes.

Things would take a wilder turn: fashion was bitten by reptiles. Adolfo of Emme was just one example. His cloche was a rather unconventional pairing of black snake with a black hair-seal brim. Cobra and water snake were other millinery favorites, along with suede, kidskin, and capeskin. Alligator and crocodile shoes (real or faux) were other de rigueur items.

Other exaggerated, ultrafeminine accessories were catalogued in *Vogue*'s description of a hat, "a huge black silk cabbage rose drenched in veiling (through which might be seen lots of earring, very little hair, and as many extra eyelashes as can be batted comfortably against the veiling)." The

all-flower chapeau still held its own, virtually unaltered from the wig-toques of the 1950s. Petals carpeted the entire head, grown on a light foundation of tulle, veiling, mesh, or hair. Swim caps copied the same floral fantasy—in rubber.

"One of our national concerns today is that women are losing their femininity," whined the *Ladies' Home Journal* in 1962. Superficially, there was reason to worry. That year Yves Saint Laurent opened his own house with streetwear inspiration: the unisex chic of a menswear peacoat, and a lizard windbreaker. Casual dress crept in, and *Vogue* described the formal, four-inch needle-heeled shoes as "the kiss of death." Tweed still held for day but now it was worn in the evening as a skirt, along with sweater tops hung with a black blizzard of jet paillettes.

While the knit cap continued its merry reign, the international set adopted a little item that kept their hairdo intact: a triangular silk scarf, tied under the chin. It was tied on by women from Jackie Kennedy to Brigitte Bardot, Audrey Hepburn to Queen Elizabeth. For summer, Saint Laurent did a navy or black and white dot silk scarf, which was slung over a kind of fitted headband or visor of straw, with the back ballooned like a snood. It was matched with a dress.

Cousin to the scarf-wrapped head was Adolfo's snug little cap—something like a baby bonnet—in wool jersey or mink-lined chiffon, tied in a bow under the chin.

Carved, tailored clothing met its match in hats of "masculine inspiration": stark, exaggerated versions of men's fedoras, Peruvian bowlers, and Edwardian toques. Fabrics could be elegant, such as Saint Laurent's silk cowboy hat. Worn through the 1960s, they gradually became a conservative standard, made up in everything from pastel straw to felt; white was the mid-1960s classic shade.

But no matter what designers did, hats kept coming off. "For the smart woman who insists on remaining hatless, the coiffure will be as importantly constructed as a hat," said *Vogue*. Constructed they were. The "postiche" —a length of hair—was the coiff aid at night, piled high, coiled into twisted, fanciful shapes, and sometimes even surmounted by a plumed headdress. To balance this superstructure of hair, skirts got shorter.

Fashion started at the bottom in 1963, with textured, quilted, sweatery stockings, Yves Saint Laurent's thigh-high croc boots, Courrèges's short white kidskin boots, and skirts that just skimmed the knee.

This was the year that Paris sought to widen its fashion market, as private client lists continued to shrink. Surely some of the conservative old guard must have been startled by couture's new note. *Vogue* described the models at Saint Laurent's fall showing as

The space-age baby look is epitomized by a bonnet originally worn with pants (label: Courrèges), OPPOSITE ABOVE. A quasipillbox of velvet with a bulky, back-fitted strap (label: Balenciaga) offers an even more modern interpretation of the 1960s, OPPOSITE BELOW. In 1969, *modern* meant lean knits with a wide-brimmed hat (by Cerrati; modeled by Jacqueline Bisset), RIGHT.

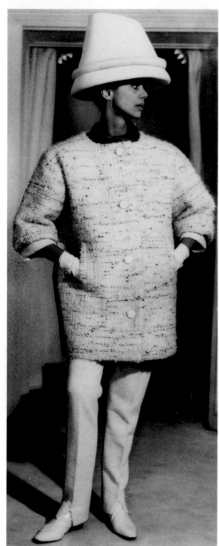

a rush of trippers from Mars, wearing jerkins and overblouses of checked wool and suede and mink with slack gold chains circling their waists, under their collars; chains rimming jaunty porkpie hats with wiglets of thick, curvy, bent Chinese hair arranged inside each one.

The daytime variation of the evening's piled-up coiffs was Vidal Sassoon's sleek straight bob with bangs. According to *Harper's Bazaar,* the face of 1963 boasted "eyebrows blotted out, lipstick faded away—the allure of an enigmatic Mona Lisa."

The helmet hat was the incarnation of the same severe chic. Expansive as a balloon, dome-shaped, strapped with a chin strap, and outfitted with a visor, it was as meticulously seamed as a football. Some helmets were as long as the face, and featured some special effects, such as a fringe of wool trim in front, like bangs. Others were plunked

on over a wrap-on jersey undercap. In stark chalk white, the masculine-style hats were mated with pale coats.

In 1965, *Vogue* introduced the term "youthquake" as the philosophy for the decade. Both 1964 and 1965 were host to a dizzying list of fashion trends, from the coolly space age to the lush romanticism of the Far East. The pace was so fast that the designer

In 1964, Courrèges built an alarming profile: a bulky coat and skinny trousers, topped by a hat shaped like a monstrous dixie cup, **LEFT**. Other designers created their own larger-than-life hattery: a puffy raffia toque, gathered into a beribboned topknot, **BELOW LEFT**; a flattened and widened chef's hat in organdy, **BELOW** (both hats by Halston, made to order, Bergdorf Goodman), and a thick-brimmed top hat of checked wool (label: Mr. John Juniors), **OPPOSITE**.

Mary Quant rocketed her entire collection of 40 pieces down the runway in a mere 14 minutes.

On the beauty front, abbreviation was also at work. Scotch tape and hair-slicking gels helped batten down tresses into short, straight, tense, geometrics. At the same time, a record number of hairpieces were used to build hairdos. Braids were intertwined with faux flowers, butterflies, jewels, even vegetables. Since both looks flourished simultaneously, hats and hairdos forged a temporary—albeit uneasy—alliance.

The 1960s was NASA's heyday: they made astronaut John Glenn the first American to orbit the planet. That event made it no surprise that fashion stayed focused on outer space. Courrèges was just one of the designers who mastered the space-age look, unveiling a collection by the same name mid-decade. His showroom—all white and as bare as an operating room—was decorated in the style associated with the space age. Courrèges seated the fashion press on square white vinyl cushions, an uncomfortable contrast to the little gilt chairs provided in more conservative showrooms. The Courrèges' models were also strikingly different: tall, tan, athletic, with freckles painted on their faces, they bounced to rock 'n' roll on the runway.

Courrèges loved pants, and his headwear had an equally streamlined

look—brimless, chin-tied baby bonnets. Edged with silver balls, or rendered in black velvet or ponyskin, the bonnet managed to be childish, sophisticated, and cleanly modern at the same time.

By 1965, Courrèges's space-age millinery had followers, although others stopped shy of his uncompromising theatricality. Adolfo did a group called "ladies in orbit," and in Paris, Marie Christiane produced a snug helmet casque inspired by the Russian cosmonauts.

Fashion's avant-gardists sided with stark, abstract hats against old-fashioned trimmings. Flowers were the exception, only if they were exaggerated. Dior's hat passed the test: it was the size of a shrub, and covered with silk anemones. Outlandish hats were stars on the covers and in the pages of *Vogue,* many of them specially made to order for just one photo.

As the scarf hat wound its way into 1965, it took on an ever-extravagant quality, prodded by the East Indian/ Schèhèrazade motif of the collections. At Dior, there were rajah coats and turbans. Harem pants billowed. Fingers, toes, shoes, and even pigtails were jeweled. Millinery responded to this splendor by coiling gauze, silk, and organza into turbans. In a burst of

A severe velour hat (label: Ohrbach's Oval Room), **OPPOSITE**, epitomizes the geometric look. A 6½-inch high origami hat is made of varnished, folded paper (label: Emme), **ABOVE RIGHT**, while metal helmets ornamented with watches premiere at a 1968 Paris fashion show (label: Paco Rabanne), **BELOW RIGHT**.

bright prints of Emilio Pucci, a fresh status symbol.

Another status accessory was the David Webb animal bracelet—zebras, leopards, etc., set with precious stones —and their imitations in rhinestone and enamel. Animal life also made an appearance on the runway in the Paris and New York collections. There were caftans of mink, suits of fake fur, and ermine dinner dresses. Fur hattery was mixed and matched with other furs as well as tailored wool coats: white mink helmets, Emme's chinchilla and velvet snood, a broadtail beanie and matching sleeveless blouse, Halston's printed dunce cap in calf stenciled to look like zebra.

Millinery continued to be featured in the prominent collections in New York and Paris, and in the heavyweight fashion magazines. However, business with the woman on the street was shaky. *Hats* bemoaned "the plight of millinery." In July 1965, New York City held an on-location publicity event designed to snap hats out of their doldrums. Milliner Edward Stutley staged a sidewalk show, sending 12 chapeau'd models down 39th Street. Improbably leading the parade ...as the poet Marianne Moore, wearing a tricorne. *The New York Times* covered the

esoteric inspiration, Diana Vreeland christened the turbans "Zamoors" after the tiny Moorish boy who carried the train of Madame du Barry. "Try a thousand windings and wrappings and tyings of turbans and scarves," she coaxed. Halston created a spectacular line of pillboxes, crowned and chintied with voluminous kerchiefs in matching geometric print silk.

In 1965, the mania for the total look of coordinated fashions launched a match game. Op Art patterns, stripes, foulards, and menswear checks covered everything from stockings to sweaters, skirts to gloves and shoes. At the dizzy peak of style: an outfit of striped stockings, houndstooth print mod shirt with white collar, matching kerchief, and a white vinyl miniskirt.

There were more scarf tricks. Hats became half-and-half numbers, fronted with a smooth straw cloche, backed with a silk scarf that bow-tied at the nape. Silk scarves were even worn under straw coolie hats. The scarf also worked alone, notably the parrot-

Silk swathed over pillboxes made an exotic frame for the extravagantly made-up face (by Halston), **ABOVE LEFT**. John Lennon, with the other Beatles, models his signature cap, **OPPOSITE ABOVE**. The snood of print silk drapes over a straw toque (label: Yves Saint Laurent), **OPPOSITE RIGHT**, and organza settles over a stiff net base (label: Adolfo), **OPPOSITE FAR RIGHT**.

event, and orders "poured in like crazy." Nice try, but it's doubtful whether the elderly Ms. Moore was the right authority figure to convince the youthquake generation that millinery was truly "with it."

To judge from magazine copy, the leg and the armhole ruled fashion in 1966. For the lower limbs, beset by the still-climbing mini, there was bronze leg makeup or white tights. For the upper limbs, the well-cut armhole persisted, Chanel's fabled legacy. While the establishment was carrying on about fine tailored details, a few couturiers launched their own revolution with ready-to-wear lines, such as Yves Saint Laurent's Rive Gauche.

Rock 'n' roll and the unisex look made headway and headlines. The quintessential beauty was described as "almost an affront to femininity, really," with "shoulderblades you could shave with"; she was the model Twiggy, and she had the body—and the face—of the year. Beauty for 1966 was hailed as "one thousand per cent faked up, engineered from extended crown down to lacquered toe." Silver colored the space age, even pearlizing makeup.

The astronaut bonnets and cosmonaut-inspired casques vanished, while halter tops, cutouts, and bareness remained. The starkness of the Courrèges style was lost in space by 1967. "A hard line seems démodé," preached Diana Vreeland. The wild geometry of prints was rampant on clothing and millinery; dizzy Op Art prints, checks, bull's-eyes, and awning stripes, as well as tiny florals in traditional or eye-jogging colors. Millinery

also translated pattern into unusual materials: mink and other furs were worked in stripes, checks, and even Op patterns.

When the modern style had run its course, the romantic look took over. By the fall of 1967, it was full-blown, pulled from sources as diverse as London's Biba boutique designs, the film *War and Peace,* Yves Saint Laurent's collection, and the hippies. Fashion magazines were heavy on the large velvet picture hat, but the style was ignored by most milliners. They produced hats that were masculine in inspiration, a safe complement to the complete masculine ensemble. The unisex hippie-inspired hattery included a raw-looking, big and floppy-brimmed suede hat, stitched together by hand. Beads, rawhide strings, macramé, flowers, or American Indian silverwork was wound around the band.

The ubiquitous cap for the mid-1960s was lifted from the Beatles: a flat, visored pull-on, editioned in everything from corduroy to print cotton to wool and canvas. Along with the Beatles cap (a few dollars at army surplus stores), a skinny ribbed sweater and hip-slung pants or a miniskirt made up the teenage uniform.

Hair was still considered a major accessory. Accommodating the wig boom, stores added wig sections to the millinery department. At the J.L. Hudson store in Detroit, wigs were available in 37 colors, priced from $150 to $200; hairpieces were priced at $35 to $80. J.C. Penney admitted that more than a quarter of its millinery sales were actually wigs, falls, and hairpieces.

The new radicalism of the 1960s was represented by a version of the cowboy hat, in plastic, complete with plastic ties and a brim rolled up at each side (label: Courrèges), **TOP.** By the end of the decade, the arrival of the scarf-wrapped head signaled millinery's doom, as seen in the pages of *Vogue,* **ABOVE.**

Despite the wig boom, *Women's Wear Daily* ran several front-page features in the spring of 1967, lauding the return of the hat. Millinery imports from Paris at Ohrbach's were sold out, even priced at $100. To accommodate customers, special wig orders were

taken, with delivery in two or three weeks.

A handful of milliners stepped along with fashion's "happening" avant garde. Sally Victor dusted off her vocabulary to create a line called "Top Gear," which featured berets in pencil-striped piqué with red patent leather visors, paper hats, and floppy numbers in fluorescent organza. Another more practical innovation—a nod to the travel-by-jet mania that infected the 1960s—was the packable hat. Soft cloches and toques could be folded in half and packed in a suitcase, other hats came with removable brims, and Paulette's two-piece linen hat buttoned together.

Most old school milliners were only marginally affected by youthquake fashions. The standards continued to be glamorous picture hats and toppers suitable for the mother of the bride. Entertainer Dinah Shore, former recipient of the Golden Hat Award, gave a speech at the Spring/Summer Millinery Institute show in 1967. As reported by *Hats,* Ms. Shore remarked that hats were important to her, and she loved to wear them, "even though it isn't easy in California." Although her remark was probably no surprise, the collective heart of the millinery industry must have sunk at her less than positive remark.

Long and lean was the shape for 1969; "string it out for all it's worth," urged *Vogue.* Fashion did just that, though the midiskirt was rejected in the process. The lean survivors were the string-bean crocheted vests, pullovers, pants, the long coats and skirts with their string-fringed scarves

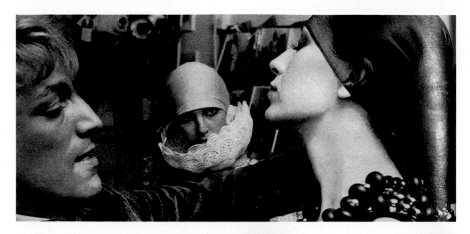

shaking down to the ankle. Hair straightened out, too, progressing from the George Washington ponytail of 1968 to a long, noncurly look, and finally to the yanked-back severity of a wrapped chignon, late in 1969.

The scarf was the last word for the 1960s. It was accepted as a fashion item because of its theatrical style, its casualness ("not-really-a-hat"), and its associations with the counterculture. The most popular scarves were in silk or cotton, with a printed pattern (paisley and other Indian prints or tapestry) or a status signature label. They were simply worn bandaged across the forehead and knotted in the back. Hair was covered or flailed free. Giorgio di Sant'Angelo became famous for the artistry of his wrapped heads. At Dior's spring 1969 show, the models wore fringed scarves, tied pirate or gypsy style, with the ends loose down their backs. The neat look of the little head was executed in other ways, too, with rough, hand-knit tams, cloches, and matching skinny scarves. In summer, there were crocheted raffia cloches and snoods.

In his spring 1969 collection, Courrèges kept the head small, plopping bobbed Dynel wigs in brilliant green,

Millinery was no match for the combination of funky street-style and the increasingly casual dress mode. As the 1960s progressed, simple head coverings replaced constructed hats. Wrap master Giorgio di Sant'Angelo twists an organza scarf around a model's head in 1969.

orange, or blue on all of his models. Pierre Cardin still showed a white vinyl chin-strapped helmet—which looked hopelessly old-fashioned.

Couture didn't make a significant contribution to the hat landscape, nor did the millinery industry; street fashion set the style. On the runway, Yves Saint Laurent matched every one of his 38 pantsuits, tunic dresses over pants, and midcalf coats with pants with a mushroom-shaped straw or felt hat. Saint Laurent made no distinction between headwear for day or evening; the same hat also served evening dresses.

Fur still growled around fashion in 1968 and 1969, essentially unchanged from early in the decade. A puffy topper of fluffy fur, such as fox, was a standard. Adolfo—who had added clothing to his repertoire—came up with an odd getup: a nearly floor-length dirndl skirt, vest, and tam, all in fur.

Patchwork was another material that was the darling of the hour. *Vogue* described it as "snips and scraps of spangled plaid and prints, jeweled and embroidered calicoes and silks, plain-as-pie pieces all plied and pieced together in a glorious crazy quilt of color and design . . . the patchwork shirt-dress-to-the-ankle to the dress for evening." Patchwork graced Beatles caps and berets, floppy brimmers, and cloches. Influenced by the Art Deco trend, geometric prints were patchworked onto jersey cloches with felt appliqués and matched with a muffler.

While patchwork crossed over into high fashion, the establishment viewed the "do-it-yourself," hippie look as a complete breakdown of good taste. "Head" shops and counterculture boutiques sold handicraft supplies for the macramé, beaded or braided leather strips worn across the forehead or tied around the crown of a hat. Black felt Navajo hats and clumsy brimmers stitched from thick leather kept perfect company with another unisex item: the ubiquitous fringed poncho.

The 1960s delivered the coup de grace to fashion conventions. Even the magic of a designer name, which licensing spread over everything from pens to luggage, failed to revive the hat as a desirable accessory. It was a sign of the times when the redoubtable Mr. John launched a line of wigs and wiglets. Each wig box carried the celebrated "Mr. John" signature in gold letters—the same proud inscription that had graced his hatboxes for years. The gesture was clearly a milliner's bow to the competition.

John-Frederics

There were two designing minds behind "John-Frederics": John Harburger and Frederic Hirst. Together, they launched the company around 1930 in New York, creating hats for the social world, films *(Gone With the Wind),* and film stars (Marlene Dietrich, Gloria Swanson). Apparently, John was the millinery showman, famous for his "firework flow of imagination" and the "maddening, but becoming whimsy" of his hats. "People say he laughs and laughs as he fits a woman into a coal-scuttle and makes her like it," fretted *Vogue* in 1940. In 1938, John featured a coffin filled with Paris-designed "miniature" hats at his show, proclaiming the death of that style.

John-Frederics inaugurated a new showroom in 1939, a fantasy decorated by Robsjohn-Gibbings. The fitting rooms were a pair of floor-to-ceiling birdcages. The entryway featured a stack of Civil War cannonballs, soldier's capes, helmets, sabers, drums, and flags—all to remind women they wore their headgear in a masculine world.

When Harburger and Hirst went their separate ways, the name took on new implications. The John-Frederics name continued, appearing on gloves, stockings, hairnets, scarfs, stoles, Golden Arrow cologne for men, and clothing for men and women. John also produced millinery under the labels Fredoras, Charmers, Sweet Young Things, and Mr. Fred.

Veiling

Even as late as the end of the 1940s, the manufacture of veiling was still labor-intensive, conducted by highly skilled craftspeople according to age-old methods. First, a veil pattern was transferred onto a chart, then punched into cardboard cards. The holes in the cardboard guided rayon, cotton, or silk threads through the machine, which twisted and crisscrossed them according to the pattern. The workers—called "twist hands"—nursed the 3,000 to 4,000 brass bobbins of thread.

The woven veil "webs" came off the machine undyed, unsized, and in tremendously wide and long bands. The bands had a binding edge on the sides, and a path of threads linked each separate section of veil. The webs were placed in huge vats of color to dye; the finest veiling was dyed by hand in a process that originated with the ancient Egyptians.

To give them body, the veils were dressed with a thin gummy solution, then stretched. Next, the veil sections were cut apart, and the loose ends clipped. Finally, the veiling was run between heated rollers, which gave it a glossy surface.

Hat Blocks

Each and every woven or stitched hat has a double: the hat block, which is its exact replica in wood or metal. The creation of the hat block (or die) is a laborious and ancient process. First, a perfectly detailed copy of the hat is made in willow. A copy of the willow model is then painstakingly whittled by hand in plaster. Next, the plaster model is cast in aluminum. The felt hat body is "blocked" or fit on the finished aluminum die. Wooden blocks are made in a similar way from specially selected hardwoods.

It wasn't until 1939 that a block with a removable crown was designed; the top could be taken on or off to create multiple hat sizes and styles.

In the 1800s, New England manufacturers produced practically all the blocks for the American millinery industry. Their job was simply to make the blocks in a style determined by the hat manufacturers. Around 1929, the blockmakers began to usurp the hat manufacturer's role, sending their own fashion scouts to Paris and London to copy the latest millinery, which enabled them to design their own hats in-house.

Halston

After Halston's death in 1990, there was a squabble about exactly who created the original pillbox hat, worn by Jacqueline Kennedy to her inauguration as First Lady in 1961. Both Halston and Oleg Cassini claimed it. However, scribbled in the margins of a letter the former First Lady sent to Bergdorf Goodman, she sketched several pillbox style hats, plus the observation, "I am afraid these hats will pauperize me." Since Halston designed millinery for Bergdorf's at the time, the honors go to him.

Born in Des Moines, Iowa, in 1932, Halston abbreviated his name from Roy Halston Frowick. His first millinery venture was a shop in Chicago's Ambassador Hotel in the 1950s. Following a stint on staff at Lilly Daché in New York City, Halston became Bergdorf Goodman's star milliner in 1958. His hats were made to order for customers, and he also created special hats just for *Vogue* photographs.

As millinery waned, Halston turned his talents to clothing, opening his own boutique at Bergdorf's in 1966. "Making hats is tremendously good training for being a dress designer. You learn to think in three dimensions, so your dresses have a sculptural quality," he observed to *Esquire* in 1975. His streamlined womenswear became the style for the 1970s: cashmere sweatshirts, streamlined jersey dresses, flannel pants. Halston himself was a model of urbanity, described as "the kind of man who makes a lot of men uncomfortable because he is so fastidious."

As his fame increased, Halston became a member of the Studio 54 crowd, hanging out with Liza Minnelli, Mick and Bianca Jagger, and Andy Warhol. In 1972, he opened a Madison Avenue boutique; the next year, he sold his name to a conglomerate, which brought about the downfall of his fashion empire.

Felt and the Felt Hat

Felt has been the milliner's staple for centuries. Even the ancient Romans made headwear fashioned from a type of primitive felt. Although felt-producing equipment has become more sophisticated, the process has remained about the same. Animal fur (beaver, otter, mink, rabbit) is used for top-quality felt; less expensive felt is created from recycled wood scraps. Both types are made in the same way.

First, fleece is scraped from the animal skins. To produce different grades of felt, long and short hairs are mixed together in varying proportions, a tricky process that requires expert knowledge. Enough fur or wool for a single hat (from two to five ounces) is packed into a tiny box. A machine spews the fur evenly over a thin, perforated metal cone, creating a hat body which is three times larger than the finished hat. A wet cloth is placed over it. To shrink the hat body, the cone is dipped in boiling water and dried by hand-rolling it on a table. The dipping and rolling process is repeated; each time, the fur is matted closer together and the texture of the felt improves.

For color, the hat bodies are boiled in dye for hours, dried, then soaked in shellac and alcohol or alkali. Next, the dry hat bodies are stretched over a block shaped like the hat crown. Brims are stretched separately. Soft felt hats have a different treatment; after the machine-blocking, they are steamed and shaped by hand over a shaped die, then ironed. A cold-water press finishes the job.

A versatile material, felt can take on multiple finishes, mimicking suede, chamois, velvet, and animal skins. To create a bouclé or pebbled surface, the nap is raised and then curled into fine or heavy knots, either by machine or hand. Velour and soleil are a pair of popular felts, made from long-cut rabbit fur. For a velour surface, the nap is raised straight up with a steel brush, then sheared with electric clippers. Soleil is created by combing the nap, and then ironing it, creating a lasting gloss. Since these processes are done by hand, soleil and velour felt are expensive.

Lilly Daché

In a 1942 profile, *The New Yorker* characterized milliner Lilly Daché as left-handed, heavily perfumed, and prone to "shriek over a mistake, or croon over a triumph." Daché even had bells on her ankles. When her nerves were all on edge during a union strike, Daché wore little bells to warn her workers of her approach; at the sound, the women would assume a calm state, forestalling a Daché tantrum. Daché reigned as America's queen of hats for 42 years.

Daché was famed for her draped turbans, which she made directly on the customer's head. "I would talk to the woman, ask her where she planned to wear the hat, what kind of dress she would wear it with," Daché later explained. "If she thought her nose was too long, I would make a hat with a brim and pull it down so you couldn't see the nose much."

Daché opened her doors in New York in 1926, just two years after leaving Paris and an apprenticeship at Reboux. From there, she moved to a succession of bigger and better shops and locations. In 1937, Daché was the first milliner to occupy an entire building, at 78 East 56th Street. Hats and 150 workers filled the first seven floors; Daché lived on the top two, in a "palazzo" with Chinese statues and semiprecious jewels hammered into the front door knocker. One salon was upholstered in leopard; there was a gold fitting room (for brunettes) and a silver fitting room (for blondes). The atmosphere was what *The New Yorker* called "the Daché millinery madhouse."

Sealed in a bronze time capsule inside the cornerstone of her building were fashion magazines, champagne, documents, a copy of her first hat, and a live horned toad, which Daché assumed would survive for 100 years. The toad never got the chance, thanks to Daché's public relations scheme. She had a friend call the ASPCA and complain about the toad's entombment. With no little drama, the cornerstone was reopened and the toad disinterred. Daché's showmanship was equal to that of her patronesses: she created hats for Joan Crawford, Carole Lombard, and Marlene Dietrich.

Daché's collections were also dramatic events. In 1942, Daché mingled with guests at her fashion shows, clad in a black dress topped with a bright pink apron. Hatted models paraded onstage, while other women squirted clouds of Daché's signature scents, Dashing and Drifting, on the crowd.

That year, Daché's hats were available in 42 stores across the country and sales topped $.5 million dollars. Prices were high; from $35 to $500 (for a hat of unborn lamb). Daché also experimented with less esoteric materials, such as cotton jute and kitchen twine. She did a collection of black hats as a gesture of mourning when Paris fell in 1940.

In the 1950s, "Mlle Lilly" and "Dachettes"—two less expensive millinery lines—were introduced. By then, Lilly had also put her name on cosmetics, stockings, gloves, wallets, women's clothing, men's shirts and ties, jewelry, and furs, as well as a branch store in Chicago and two books.

It was a sign of changing times when Daché turned her attention to another kind of headcovering in the late 1950s: a beauty salon. Hairdresser Kenneth Battell (who still operates the Kenneth salon in New York) had his start in Daché's establishment. So did Halston Frowick, an apprentice milliner, later famous simply as Halston.

When she closed her salon in 1968, loyal actress Loretta Young showed up to clean the shelves of the last 30 hats. Daché died in 1989.

Sally Victor
In 1962, rival milliner Mr. John described Sally Victor as a "brain picker." Arch rival milliner Lilly Daché gallantly saluted her as "exceptionally gifted in the use of color." Victor credited herself with a photographic memory and theft: stealing inspiration for her chapeaux from masterpiece paintings. Said Victor to the *Saturday Evening Post,* "What I pinch are marketable ideas, easily translated into high fashion." Translate and pinch she did. Under pressure, Victor designed up to 30 hats a day, and a total of 2,000 models a year. In 1956, Victor was the first milliner to win a coveted Coty fashion award. By 1959, she ran the largest American millinery company. Victor's creations were priced from $55 to $90, and up to $1,000 for hats with fur or jewelry. Her lower-priced numbers, sold under the "Sally V" label, went for $15 to $35. Clients included Queen Elizabeth II and the best-dressed Babe Paley; Prince Rainier bought an Easter bonnet for Princess Grace from the Victor showroom. First Lady Mamie Eisenhower wore Victor's "airwave" chapeau to Ike's first inauguration. Victor also had designs on another presidential wife—Jackie Kennedy. Photos of the hat-shunning First Lady with only a kerchief tied over her head moved Victor to moan, "How can she do that to another Democrat?"

A native of Pennsylvania, Victor worked as a stockroom girl and then a designer in Macy's millinery department in the early 1920s. After marriage to a wholesale milliner, she gradually took over his business, changing the firm's name to Sally Victor in 1934.

Victor had firm thoughts on the relationship between women and their headwear. "If a hat doesn't do anything for a woman, she ought to wear a shawl." On the relationship between husbands and hats, "Criticizing a hat is a husband's psychological outlet," mused Victor. "It's a way he has for letting off steam. What he feels about his wife he says about her hat. If a girl's husband criticizes her new hat, she shouldn't blame the designer. She should consult a lawyer."

glossary of hat types

beret

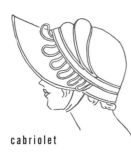

Breton sailor

cabriolet

cloche

aigrette   Stiff, floating feathers used to decorate hats. *See* EGRET.

Alpine   A man's casual hat, first introduced in the late 1890s, adapted from Austrian Tyrolean and Bavarian models. Usually made of felt, with a slightly peaked crown and upturned brim in back.

babushka   A triangular scarf worn around the head, with the ends tied under the chin. From the Russian word for grandmother.

bagnolette   A lightweight fabric hood, wired to stand away from the face. First worn in the 18th century.

bakou   A Chinese straw woven from the fiber of the Philippine buri palm.

ballibuntal   A fine millinery straw, woven from the buri palm. Similar to BAKOU, but smoother.

beret   A round, brimless, soft bouffant cap. Originally worn by Basque men.

bicorne   A hat turned up in back and front and held together at the sides, forming points over each ear. Men's headwear during and after the French Revolution, ornamented with a cockade.

biretta   A stiff or soft cap with a flat top, often with four corners. Worn by Roman Catholic priests, bishops, and cardinals.

boater   A hard straw hat with a flat crown and flat brim, decorated with a plain ribbon band around the crown. Popular for men in the late 19th century. Also called a CANOTIER.

body hat   A hat made all in one piece—not fashioned from sewn strips—of straw, felt, or wool.

bolero   Similar to the MATADOR, with an evenly turned-up brim and revers.

bonnet   A close-fitting, brimmed headdress tied under the chin with ribbon strings. Most popular during the reign of Louis Philippe, 1830–1848.

bowler   A hard felt hat with a domed crown and narrow rolled brim, usually black, high fashion for men around 1871. Originally worn with a formal riding habit, and by English businessmen. Similiar to the DERBY.

Breton sailor   A sailor hat with upturned brim.

bumper   A hat with a thick, rolled-back brim; crowns may be in various styles.

busby   A tall, cylindrical hat, sometimes in black fur, originally worn by hussars and certain regiments of the British army.

cabriolet   A huge, deep-brimmed bonnet with elaborate ribbon bows and plumes. Worn in the early 1800s.

calotte   1. A small black cap worn by Roman clergy. 2. A cap worn under a beret.

canotier   *See* BOATER.

cap   Any close-fitting headgear.

capeline   A hat with a wide, floppy brim fitted to a snug crown.

capote   A shallow-crowned bonnet topped with a kerchief. First introduced in 1806.

cartwheel   A hat with an exaggerated wide brim and a low crown. Frequently made of straw. *See also* LEGHORN.

casque   A snug, helmet-shaped hat.

cellophane   A manmade, paperlike material that is transparent and waterproof.

charlotte or **Charlotte Corday**   A round, soft fabric cap with a gathered, face-framing frill, tied on with a ribbon band. From the cap worn by Charlotte Corday, French patriot who assassinated the terrorist Marat during the Revolution.

chechia   A tall cylindrical hat, similar to a FEZ.

cloche   A tight-fitting, deep-crowned hat with a narrow brim, worn pulled down over the eyebrows. Introduced in the 1920s. From the French for bell.

coolie   A shallow, round hat with a center peak and slanting sides, made of straw and other materials. From the Chinese *kuli,* an unskilled worker.

cornette   A cone-shaped hat tied under the chin.

cossack   A tall, brimless fur hat, worn by Russian cavalrymen.

cowboy hat   A wide-brimmed felt hat with a tall creased or uncreased crown and a brim rolled up on the sides and dipped in front. Also called TEN GALLON HAT.

crin   The French term for horsehair.

derby   *See* BOWLER. A hat named for the Earl of Derby and the English Derby horse race.

doll hat   A miniature, ''doll-sized'' hat, frequently worn pitched over the forehead and secured

116

doll hat

fontenage or tower

halo hat

Juliet cap

with elastic, combs, or hatpins. Popular in the late 1930s.

Dolly Varden   A straw hat, worn tilted forward over the forehead. After a character from the Charles Dickens novel *Barnaby Rudge*.

dunce cap   A tall, pointed, cone-shaped hat without a brim.

egret   Feathers obtained from several varieties of heron.

Empress Eugénie   A small hat, worn pitched forward over one side of the face. Revived in 1931. From Empress Eugénie, wife of Napoleon III (1852–1870).

fedora   A felt hat with a medium-sized brim and a crown with a front-to-back crease. Originally a man's hat, it became popular in 1882 after Sardou's play *Fedora*.

felt   A nonwoven fabric of wool, fur, or hair, matted together by pressure.

fez   A tall, cylindrical felt hat with a flat top, ornamented with a tassel dangling from the center top. Named for the town of Fez in Morocco.

fontenage or **tower**   A tall, fanlike headdress of stiffened lace, worn in the late 17th century. Originated by the Duchess de Fontenages, a court favorite of Louis XIV.

Gainsborough   A low-crowned, very broad-brimmed hat of velvet, beaver, or straw, trimmed with feathers. Hatpins were plunged through a bandeau on the underside of the brim, which slightly raised the hat. It reached its maximum width in 1907.

Garbo   A crushable, high-crowned hat with a floppy brim that could be turned up in front. Frequently made of felt. Made popular by Greta Garbo in the 1930s. *See also* SLOUCH HAT.

gigolo   A high-crowned hat with a center crease and narrow brim, turned up in back and down in front. Similar to the FEDORA. Fashionable around 1926.

gypsy hat   A wide-brimmed straw hat, tied down with streamers.

halo hat   A medium- to wide-brimmed hat worn toward the back of the head, framing the face.

harlequin   A hat with a wide, turned-up brim and oblique sides.

helmet   A close-fitting cap with sides extending over the ears.

homburg   A man's stiff felt hat with a narrow rolled brim and a lengthwise-creased crown. Worn from the 1870s on formal occasions. Edward VII, when Prince of Wales, popularized the Homburg by his visits to Homburg in Germany.

hood   Soft headwear, draped close around the head, neck, and shoulders.

Juliet cap   A small skullcap, frequently edged with pearls.

leghorn   1. A wide-brimmed hat with a high crown, heavily decorated in front with ribbon and flowers. Popular around 1825. Usually made from woven "leghorn" straw. 2. A finely woven, finely ridged straw. The finest-grade leghorn straw is deep cream; it is also available in black and various colors. From the English name for Livorno, Italy, the straw's town of export.

marabou   Soft, downlike feathers of a species of stork.

marquis   A TRICORNE with a contrasting brim binding, usually trimmed with a cockade. Popular during the reign of Louis XV (1643–1715).

Mary Stuart   A small, snug cap with a heart-shaped "widow's peak" over the forehead, fitting closely over the back of the head. Named after Mary Queen of Scots.

matador   A stiff fabric hat shaped like a bull's head, with two "horns" and a round forehead. Worn by Spanish and Mexican bullfighters.

merry widow   A picture hat with a wide, exaggerated brim and lavish decoration. After the early-1900s stage play of the same name.

milan straw   One of the finest Italian straws, woven in a closely ribbed pattern.

mitre   A bishop's headdress, made of brocade, sometimes jeweled.

mob cap   A soft fabric cap gathered with a ruffle around its lower edge.

Mountie hat   A wide-brimmed hat with a high-peaked crown, divided into four folds. Worn by forest rangers and the Royal Canadian Mounted Police.

mousquetaire or **musketeer**   A tall-crowned, wide-brimmed hat, often ornamented with feather plumes. Associated with *The Three Musketeers* by Dumas père.

mushroom   A hat with a deep, often puffed crown and a medium brim.

open crown   A wide-brimmed hat without a crown.

opera   A man's tall silk hat with a collapsible

pillbox

profile hat

tricorne

turban

crown, worn for dress occasions. Created in 1823 by a Frenchman, Antoine Gibus.

paille dentelle   Straw woven in a lace design.

Pamela bonnet   A variation of the POKE-BONNET, with a curving brim that revealed the cheeks. Popular around 1835.

panama   The original "panama" hats were braided by hand from the *jipijapa* plant in Ecuador. The term now includes any man's straw summer hat.

pancake hat   A flat beret.

Phrygian cap   A helmet-shaped hat, curved down over the ears.

picture hat   See LEGHORN.

pillbox   A brimless, circular hat of medium height, worn forward or backward on the head.

pokebonnet   A bonnet with a deep bill projecting in front, fastened under the chin with ties.

porkpie   1. A man's snap-brim hat, flat-topped, with a crease circling the crown. Made of straw, fabric, or felt. 2. A woman's hat of the 1860s, with a low, flat crown and narrow, turned-up brim.

profile hat   A hat with the brim turned up on one side, exposing only the profile.

Quaker   A low-crowned, wide-brimmed hat, adopted by the Quakers.

raffia   A vegetable fiber woven into wide or narrow flat braids.

Robin Hood   A felt or suede hat with the crown shaped to a soft point, tucked or folded. Trimmed with a quill feather, set at an angle. After the traditional English 12th-century outlaw.

safari hat   A lightweight straw or fabric hat with a medium-sized brim. Similar to a pith helmet, but with a shallower, round crown.

sailor   1. A man's hat of white duck fabric with a gored crown and close-fitting, upturned brim, worn over the forehead or on the back of the head. 2. A woman's shallow-crowned straw hat with a straight brim and plain ribbon trim around the crown. Worn since the 1860s; popular in 1890s for casual wear. *See also* BOATER; SKIMMER.

sisal   A fine straw, made of fibers from the agave plant.

skimmer   A SAILOR or BOATER hat with an exaggerated shallow crown and wide brim.

skullcap   A shallow, small, brimless fabric cap, fit closely to the top of the head.

slouch hat   A flexible hat, similar to the FEDORA, with a slightly wider, flexible brim. *See also* GARBO.

snood   A woven or knotted net, worn to cover or contain the hair.

sombrero   A Mexican hat with a tall, slightly tapered crown and large, upturned brim. From the Spanish *sombre,* meaning to shade.

Sou'wester   A hat with a sectioned, dome-shaped crown and broad, stitched brim. Originally made in yellow oiled silk. First worn by New England fishermen.

Stetson   An American manufacturer's trade name for a man's hat.

sugarloaf   A tall, exaggerated hat with a tapering crown.

swagger hat   A casual hat with a medium-sized brim, turned down in front. Worn by men and women.

tam-o'-shanter   A wide, flat beret with a tight headband and a puff tassel on top. Originally Scottish. After the hero of a poem by Robert Burns.

ten gallon hat   An extra-tall felt cowboy hat without a creased crown. Similar to SOMBRERO.

top hat   A man's tall hat of silk or brushed beaver cloth, with a slightly rolling narrow brim. Unlike the OPERA hat, it is not collapsible.

toque   A small, close-fitting brimless cap of various styles. From the Italian *tocca,* a cap.

toyo   Thin, strong tissue paper, rolled and woven to imitate millinery straws. From the Japanese *toyo,* meaning Far East.

tricorne   A medium-crowned hat with the brim turned up on three sides. Introduced as a man's hat around 1690.

trilby   A man's soft felt-brimmed hat. After a character in George du Maurier's novel *Trilby.*

turban   1. A headdress or scarf wound directly around the head, or around a cap. 2. A small hat, either brimless or with the brim closely turned up against the crown. Originally worn by men in the East. From the Turkish *turband.*

velours   French for velvet.

Watteau hat   See PICTURE HAT. Associated with the French painter Antoine Watteau (1684–1721).

wimple   A loose fabric, pinned to the top of the head and draped under the chin. A second piece of fabric extends from the forehead over the back of the head.

[a guide for hat collectors]

Even if you are just beginning to collect, vintage hats are still widely available. At grass roots level, there are yard, estate, and tag sales, flea markets, and thrift shops. Look under headings for Clothing Bought and Sold, Vintage, Secondhand, or Used Clothing in your local yellow pages. For the collector interested in a pre-edited selection, vintage clothing stores are a more upscale source.

Flea markets and antique expositions across the country feature vintage clothing and millinery. The largest shows, generally held in fall and early spring, include the Pier Show, New York City; the Vintage Fashion Exposition, Oakland, California; and the Brimfield Market, Brimfield Massachusetts.

See Directory, page 120, for addresses of newsletters, millinery suppliers, and shops.

Evaluating a Hat
To determine whether a hat will hold up to wearing, check the type and condition of the material. Stiff silks, like taffeta, tend to crack and wear out sooner than softer silks. Velvet is longer lasting than most other fabrics. To check for quality, fold over a corner; the best velvet has a thick pile and shows less of the fabric backing underneath. Fur can also be given the fold test to determine whether it has dried out. To evaluate the quality of a hat made of woven straw, hold it up to the light to check for patches, knots, and holes. The color should also be checked: if a hat has faded, it has lost its flexibility. Finally, lightly pinch the brim: it should bend easily, not crunch or crackle.

Detective work is required for a millinery investment. The inside of a hat is the first clue. Pre- or early-1920s creations can usually be dated by the presence of a wire frame structure, some kind of sewn-in stiffening, and a handsewn lining, often of black fabric. In later decades, there was less hand-done detail work in hat construction. Signs of a less-than-the-best quality chapeaux: glued (rather than sewn on) decorations, and/or no lining, hat band, or label.

A hat's age and value can be determined by the label. A famous milliner or couturier label makes a hat a collectible, and sometimes even a museum-quality piece. Better-quality hats generally carry at least two labels: one from the store and one from the milliner. Older hats are also embellished with a smaller tag identifying head size. Top-of-the-line stores carried the most stylish headgear; though many of these stores are no longer in business, their labels are a testament to their taste. A sampling of prominent and now defunct stores includes: Hattie Carnegie, B. Altman, Russek's, Arnold Constable, Best & Co., Jay-Thorpe, and Franklin Simon.

Labels were also bold enough to note that the hats they graced were unabashed reproductions. For example, a 1950s straw boater carried two labels: one read "copy of a Chanel original" and the other "Saks Fifth Avenue." Other designers split their lines. A Christian Dior hat for the American market is labeled "Christian Dior New York" to distinguish it from a Paris-made original. Mass market hats were often simply labeled with a small "union made" tag. However, even without a famous name, a hat can be valuable for its workmanship, materials, and design.

Hat Care and Cleaning
Common sense is the best guide for the care of vintage hats. Purists will never wear their vintage millinery; less strict collectors will wear it only over clean hair.

Purist or not, rain is something to avoid: felt and other fabrics can shrink and spot, glue and stiffener can dissolve, and straw can collapse. To remedy fallout from a downpour, reshape the hat over crumpled paper or a bunched-up cloth and allow it to dry very gradually. Never set a wet hat on its brim or hang it up. If the hat has a leather band, turn it out, and set it down on the "platform" so that air can circulate evenly.

Before cleaning a hat, identify the material. Felt hats can be difficult to distinguish, since they can be wool or fur felt. (Look for a "wool" or "felt" stamp inside the crown.)

To maintain their luster and shape, wool felt hats should be treated with an iron and brushed, never steamed. First, stuff the crown of the hat with a wadded cloth, such as a hand towel. Place a slightly dampened cotton sheet over the hat, and gently smooth the surface with an iron set on a moderate temperature. Frequently check progress under the pressing cloth, and redampen if necessary. Follow with a brushing: for light-colored hats, use a brush with blond bristles; darker hats take dark bristles.

Stains can be treated in several ways. For spots and smudges not caused by a liquid, use an art gum eraser. For deeper stains, saturate the spot with dry starch or cornmeal. Let stand for several hours so that the powder is absorbed by the spot, then brush well with a stiff brush. Use very fine sandpaper on stubborn small spots.

To clean fur felt hats and make them more pliable, use a steam treatment. Hold the hat over steaming water for a few minutes. Beware: oversteaming or placing the hat too close to the water can cause it to shrink.

Hats of velvet or fur can also be gently steamed. Velvet hats should be brushed against the nap with a soft brush. Feathered hats can be misted with hairspray after a gentle steaming. Crushed ornaments, droopy ribbons, and fabric flowers can also be revived using the same technique.

For best results, have felt halts professionally cleaned by a hatter; dry cleaners can clean, but not reblock, hats. In New York City, Worth & Worth Ltd. (331 Madison Avenue, [212] 867-6058) will clean fur felt hats; New Champion Shoe Repairing & Hat Cleaning Shop (127 Greenwich Avenue, New York City) do the same for wool felt headgear.

Because they are especially fragile, straw hats are more difficult to resuscitate. Good quality panama hats can be handwashed with a pure soap and cold water. (First test the headband to make certain it is colorfast.) Gently agitate the hat in water, rinse well. Dry on a block or stuff the crown with paper or cloth. To freshen or restore a bent-out-of-shape straw hat, hold it over boiling water for a few minutes. Dry as above. Do not oversteam, since the hat glue and sizing will soften. Onionskin and cellophane straws should not be dampened; natural fiber straw can be treated damp or dry.

Leghorn straw hats can be reshaped with an iron. First, stuff the crown with cloth or paper. Lightly mist the hat with water. Place a piece of dry cloth over the hat and press until dry with an iron set on moderate temperature. Never place an iron directly on straw: it can stretch the hat and make its surface shiny.

Do not wash decorated or fabric hats: they are usually stiffened with materials that will dissolve when wet.

Storage
Ideally, hats should be stored in an environment free of light, moisture, and dust: a hat box. The outside of the hat, as well as the inside of the box should be filled with acid-free paper (see Millinery Supplies). To avoid rippling, hats should always be put away with their brims turned up.

MILLINERY SUPPLIES

Cherish
P.O. Box 941
New York, New York 10024
Museum quality padded hangers, fabric dust covers, acid-free boxes and tissue. Brochure available.

Talas
213 West 35th Street
New York, New York 10001
(212) 736-7744
Conservation supplies: acid-free tissue and boxes. Minimum order. Free catalogue available.

Helene Von Rosenfield
382 11th Street
Brooklyn, New York 11215
(718) 788-7909
Acid-free tissue and other supplies available in small quantities. Restoration work for individuals and institutions.

NEWSLETTERS

Points
Lillian Baker
15237 Chanera Avenue
Gardena, California 90249
Newsletter for International Club for Collectors of Hatpins and Hatpin Holders. Quarterly. Send SASE for information.

Textures
301 North Pomona Avenue
Fullerton, California 92632
Newsletter of the Textile and Costume Guild of the Fullerton Museum. Write for subscription, membership information.

Vintage Clothing Newsletter
Terry McCormick
P.O. Box 1422
Corvallis, Oregon 97339
Newsletter for vintage clothing collectors. $12.00 a year or $15.00 first class mail; 6 issues a year.

Federation of Vintage Fashion
P.O. Box 412
Alamo, California 94507

Vintage Fashions
900 Frederick Street
Cumberland, Maryland 21502

VINTAGE CLOTHING SHOPS

alaska

The Rage
423 G Street
Anchorage, AK 99501
907-274-7243

Sacks 36th Avenue
601 W. 36th Avenue
Anchorage, AK 99501
907-562-7227

arizona

Honey Buns
5801 North 7th Street
Phoenix, AZ 85014
602-266-4353

Sweet Charity
7607 East Mcdowell
Scottsdale, AZ 85257
602-941-1618

Yesterday's
935 North 8th Street
Phoenix, AZ 85014
602-861-9080

california

Aardvard's Odd Ark
1501 Haight Street
San Francisco, CA 94117
415-621-3141

Bizarre Bazaar
5634 College Avenue
Oakland, CA 94601
415-655-2909

Buffalo Exchange
1800 Polk Street
San Francisco, CA 94117
415-431-7733

Cheap Thrills
1217 21st Street
Sacramento, CA 95816
916-446-1366

Get Smart
239 Alamitos
Long Beach, CA 90814
213-437-1811

Ginny's Antiques Et Ct
190 Camino Real
Tustin, CA 92680
714-832-7655

Heirloom Impressions
1617 Ashby Avenue
Berkeley, CA 94703
415-843-3071
Mail order sales, and reproduction of
vintage clothing available. Send $1
and SASE.

Jet Rags
611 Melrose Avenue
Los Angeles, CA 90038
213-465-7767

Lacis
2982 Adeline Street
Berkeley, CA 94703
415-843-7178

Lakewood Millinery
1094 East Wardlow
Long Beach, CA 90814
213-427-5035

La Rue
5320 Lankershim Boulevard
North Hollywood, CA 91601
818-980-1660

Lydia the Purple Merchant
2368 High Street
Oakland, CA 94601
415-655-2909

Meow Modes for Moderns
2210 East 4th Street
Long Beach, CA 90814
213-438-8990

Now & Again
2101 L Street
Sacramento, CA 95816
916-447-9443

Pure Gold
718 State Street
Santa Barbara, CA 93111
805-962-4613

Ragtime Cowboy
5332 Lankershim Boulevard
North Hollywood, CA 91601
818-769-2072

Ragtime Cowboy
1644 North Wilcox Avenue
Hollywood, CA 90028
213-463-7811

Rare Finds
P.O. Box 6431
Santa Barbara, CA 93111
805-962-7741

Razzamatazz
1118 Magnolia
North Hollywood, CA 91601
818-980-1660

Wasteland
1660 Haight Street
San Francisco, CA 94117
415-863-3150

The Way We Wore
2238 Fillmore Street
San Francisco, CA 94115
415-346-1386

colorado

Repeat Boutique
239 Linden
"Old Town" Fort Collins, CO 80524
303-493-1039

connecticut

Ann Marie's
1569 Chapel Street
New Haven, CT 06511
203-787-1734

Casablanca
1219 Chapel Street
New Haven, CT 06511
203-789-1630

Roxie Taylor
Old Avon Village
Avon,CT
203-674-8917

Yesterday's Threads
564 Main Street
Branford, CT 06405
203-481-6452

florida

Creative Collections
527 Pineapple Street
Sarasota, FL 33577
813-951-0477

The Glass Slipper
653 Orange Street
Sarasota, FL 33577
813-951-1547

Miami Twice
6562 S.W. 40th Street
Miami, FL 33155
305-666-0127

Stock Exchange
2440 Wilton Drive
Ft. Lauderdale, FL 33305
305-564-3090

illinois

Flashy Trash
3524 North Halsted
Chicago, IL 60657
312-327-6990

Strange Cargo
3448 North Clark Street
Chicago, Il 60657
312-327-8090

indiana

Modern Times
5363 North College
Indianapolis, IN 46220
317-253-8108

Red Rose Vintage Clothing
834 East 64th at Guilford
Indianapolis, IN 46220
317-257-5016

kansas

Barb's Vintage Rose
927 Massachusetts Street
Lawrence, KS 66044
913-841-2451

Klassic Line Vintage
1422 East Douglas
Wichita, KS 67214
316-263-7662

The Orange Crate
3125 S.W. Huntoon
Topeka, KS 66603
913-296-9207

Pastense
418 West Sixth Street
Topeka, KS 66603
913-233-7107

louisiana

Jazzrags
1223 Decatur Street
New Orleans, LA 70130
504-887-4965

maryland

**Belle's Antique &
Apparel Shop**
7399 Liberty Road
Baltimore, MD 21207
301-944-9686

Dreamland
212 W. Read Street
Baltimore, MD 21207
301-727-4575

212 Somerset
P. O. Box 361
Princess Anne, MD 21853
301-651-3655

massachusetts

Atalanta
1766 Massachusetts Avenue
Cambridge, MA 02140
617-661-2673

Great Eastern Trading Company
49 River Street
Cambridge, MA 02128
617-354-5279

Reddog's
1737 Massachusetts Avenue
Cambridge, MA 02140
617-354-9676

Vintage Etc.
1796 Massachusetts Avenue
Cambridge, MA 02140
617-497-1516

michigan

Antiques on Main
115 South Main Street
Royal Oak, MI 48067
313-545-4663

minnesota

Gabrela's
1431 West Lake Street
Minneapolis, MN 55406
612-822-1512

The Corner Store
900 West Lake Street
Minneapolis, MN 55406
612-823-1270

new york

Daybreak
199 Central Avenue
Albany, NY 12206
518-434-4321

Harriet Love
412 West Broadway
New York, NY 10012
212-966-2280

The Enchanted Room
65–67 Sheather Street
Hammondsport, NY 14840
1-800-544-0198

ohio

Rick's Fashions Americain
330 Selma Road
Springfield, OH 45505
513-322-7766

oregon

Antrican
1245 Willamette
Eugene, OR 97401
503-484-5750

Avalon Antiques
318 S.W. 9th Ave
Portland, OR 97205
503-224-7156

Old Friends
1022 Willamette
Eugene, OR 97401
503-345-1414

Persona Vintage Clothing
1249 Commercial
Astor Building, Suite 205
Astoria, OR 97103
503-325-3837

Rays Ragtime
1021 S.W. Morrison
Portland, OR 97205
503-226-2616

pennsylvania

M. Klien
203 South 17th Street
Philadelphia, PA 19103
215-732-7171

Steppin' Out
10 West Mechanic Street
New Hope, PA 18938
215-862-5921

Yesterdays Delight
7 Penn's Market Rte. 202
Lahaska, PA 18931
215-794-7676

tennessee

Flash Back
2304 Central
Memphis, TN 38119
901-272-2304

Frederica's Studio Collection
990 June Road
Memphis, TN 38119
901-767-1034

The Heirloom Collection
Broad Street Antiques
211 Broad Street
Kingsport, TN 37660
615-323-4993

texas

Ahab Bowen
2614 Boll
Dallas, TX 75205
214-720-1874

Déjà Vu
2705-A 26th Street
Lubbock, TX 79410
806-799-6845

Grama's Attic
1500 West Alabama
Houston, TX 77006
713-520-1408

Puttin' On the Ritz
3113 Knox Street
Dallas, TX 75205
214-522-8030

Secondhand Rose
521 North Elm Street
Denton, TX 76201
817-566-1917

Step Back Vintage Fashion
3939 Montrose
Houston, TX 77006
713-522-7979

Vintage Rose
2610 Salem
Lubbock, TX 79410
806-793-7673

Wear It Again Sam
1411 Westheimer
Houston, TX 77006
713-523-5258

vermont

Dust and Glitter
31 Gage Street
North Mentiminster, VT 05101
802-463-4958

virginia

Bygones
2916 West Cary Street
Richmond, VA 23221
804-353-1919

Halcyon
117 North Robinson Street
Richmond, VA 23221
804-358-1311

Luxor
3001 West Cary Street
Richmond, VA 23221
804-359-6780

washington

Fritzi Ritz Vintage Clothing
3425 Fremont Place North
Seattle, WA 98188
206-633-0929

Isadora's Antique Clothing
1920½ 1st Street
Seattle, WA 98188
206-441-7711

Madame & Company
117 Yesler Way
Seattle, WA 98104
206-621-1728

Ruston Galleries
5105 North Pearl
Tacoma, WA 98407
206-759-2624

Tootsie's
609 2nd Street
Seattle, WA, 98188
206-682-0807

west virginia

Carol Ratz Vintage Clothes
Box 867 Route 44 South
Logan, WV 25601
304-752-5212

wisconsin

Flapper Alley Ltd.
1518 North Farwell Avenue
Milwaukee, WI 53202
414-276-6252

Notes

INTRODUCTION

page 9 "if you are discouraged . . ." *Harper's Bazaar*, May 1930, p. 55.

10 "The best of the new hats . . ." *Fashionable Dress*, February 1925, p. 18.

12 "some of the visiting . . ." *Hats*, September 1956, p. 1.

13 "I don't like hats," quoted in Marylin Bender, *The Beautiful People* (New York: Coward-McCann, 1967), p. 258.

"I consider that without hats . . ." *Hats*, April 1957, p. 1.

THE 20s

15 "Women today . . .;" and "rather smoke . . ." Cecil Beaton, *Book of Beauty* (London: B. T. Batsford, 1929), p. 49.

16 "a curveless similarity . . ." Carolyn Hall, *The Twenties in Vogue* (London: Octopus Books, 1983), p. 55.

"practically live in bathing suits . . ." Carolyn Hall, *The Twenties in Vogue* (London: Octopus Books), 1983, p. 86.

19 "In fact, in millinery . . ." *Dry Goods Economist*, March 1921, p. 83.

20 "The extremely wide-brimmed hat . . ." *Millinery Trade Review*, July 1922, p. 40.

"new and horrific era of dress . . ." *Millinery Trade Review*, March 1922, p. 67.

"the delightful custom . . ." *Millinery Trade Review*, November 1920, p. 62.

"One affects girlishness . . ." *Fashionable Dress*, April 1924, p. 18.

"We flatten our hair . . ." Cecil Beaton quoted in *The Twenties in Vogue*, Carolyn Hall (London: Octopus Books, 1983), p. 56.

21 "Just so long . . ." *Fashionable Dress*, April 1924, p. 6.

23 "The critics of fashion's inconsistencies . . ." *Fashionable Dress*, December 1924, p. 78.

"becomes preposterous, even grotesque . . ." *Vogue*, January 1, 1926, p. 35.

24 "Smart women no longer . . ." *Vogue*, September 15, 1927, p. 63.

"so often that one . . ." *Vogue*, January 15, 1926, p. 75.

"Women are allowed . . ." *Vogue*, September 15, 1927, p. 63.

25 "All the dictates . . ." *Dry Goods Economist*, September 22, 1928, p. 47.

"Gay colors . . ." *Vogue*, September 15, 1927, p. 79.

28 "The new silhouette . . ." *Fashionable Dress*, February 1928, p. 8.

"She has exhausted . . ." *Fashionable Dress*, November 1929, p. 5.

THE 30S

31 "If women have no wit . . ." Lilly Daché, *Talking Through My Hats* (New York: Coward-McCann, 1946), p. 167.

Esquire, June 1963, p. 43.

32 "Dress is merely . . ." *Delineator*, October 1926, p. 2.

"Bonnets, berets, sailors . . ." Cecil Beaton, *Cecil Beaton's Scrapbook* (London: B. T. Batsford, 1937), p. 62.

"no longer a question . . ." *Millinery Trade Review*, February 1935, p. 16.

"It is vulgar . . ." *Vogue*, January 15, 1930, p. 50.

"Hats are more hilarious . . ." *Fashion Arts*, December 1935, p. 25.

35 "Profiles have become . . ." *Vogue*, July 15, 1931, p. 23.

"Here's to the Princess Eugénie . . ." *Millinery Trade Review*, October 1931, p. 7

"American women recovered . . ." *Fashion Accessories*, November 1931, p. 12.

37 "One's body . . ." *Vogue*, February 1, 1934, p. 21.

38 "She is getting a little sick . . ." *Harper's Bazaar*, November 1933, p. 55.

"calculated to confuse . . ." *Fashion's Art*, December 1935, p. 25.

"Lose your nationality . . ." *Junior League Bulletin*, October 1935, p. 86.

40 "almost outnumbered . . ." *Vogue*, June 15, 1935, p. 29.

"I sell four colored hats . . ." *Contemporary Modes*, September 1935, p. 16

43 "The Depression's over . . ." *Contemporary Modes*, Paris issue, 1936, p. 12.

44 "If you are taking . . ." Carolyn Hall, *The Thirties in Vogue* (London: Octopus Books, 1983), p. 105.

"rising like crags . . ." *Harper's Bazaar*, August 1937, p. 49.

"A woman is a little . . ." *Harper's Bazaar*, September 15, 1937, p. 90.

46 "We are entering a season . . ." *Harper's Bazaar*, April 1938, p. 63.

47 "If the male populace . . ." *Millinery Trade Review*, July 1938, p. 33.

"The entire gamut . . ." quoted in *Millinery Trade Review*, September 1938, p. 24.

49 "If all the ribbons . . ." *Contemporary Modes*, June 1938, p. 25.

"hatless ones . . ." *Harper's Bazaar*, May 1938, p. 56.

"A heavy flower . . ." *Vogue*, April 15, 1939, p. 70.

50 "Swath your head . . ." *Vogue*, January 15, 1939, p. 105.

Suzy complained . . . *Contemporary Modes*, December 1939, p. 19.

THE 40s

53 "As a result of the war . . ." Christian Dior, *Dior by Dior* (London: Weidenfeld & Nicolson, 1957), p. 25.

"Women who themselves . . ." *Hats*, August 1943, p. 22.

54 "She'll be the wide awake girl . . ." *Mademoiselle*, March 1941, p. 103.

"American women are the best-dressed . . ." *Collier's*, January 1941, p. 32.

55 "She'll have loyalties . . ." *Mademoiselle*, March 1941, p. 103.

yearly hat sales . . . *The New York Times*, April 3, 1940, p. 32.

"Saks Fifth Avenue's Mr. Joseph . . ." *The New Yorker*, February 21, 1942, p. 53.

56 "The way not to look . . ." *Vogue*, January 15, 1945, p. 45.

"There is much to be said . . ." *Collier's*, February 17, 1945, p. 72.

"To the ladies . . ." *Contemporary Modes*, Easter 1942, p. 6.

59 "character, consideration . . ." *Vogue*, September 15, 1942, p. 71.

"Individuality stalks . . ." *Harper's Bazaar*, September 1942, p. 98.

62 "*Life* editors are well aware . . ." *Life*, March 23, 1942, p. 110.

68 "The clothing is arrogant . . ." *Life*, November 20, 1944, p. 47.

"Hats after V-J day . . ." *Millinery Trade Review*, August 1945, p. 2.

70 "In an epoch as somber . . ." *The New York Times*, June 13, 1965, p. 64.

"half-hair, half-hat . . ." *Vogue*, October 15, 1947, p. 65.

"does almost anything . . ." *Vogue,* August 1, 1949, p. 53.
"even those recalcitrant . . ." *Millinery Monitor,* August 1949, p. 3.

THE 50s

73 "The last year has been . . ." *The New York Times Magazine,* July 15, 1959, p. 19.
75 "I've always sympathized . . ." *The New York Times Magazine,* September 11, 1960, p. 34.
77 "evenings of canasta . . ." *Flair,* October 1950, p. 51.
"A lady never runs . . ." *Hats,* October 1951, p. 1.
"We think you will see . . ." *Vogue,* September 15, 1950, p. 21.
"I adore you . . ." *The New York Times Magazine,* January 1957, p. 24.
78 "Pair a smooth . . ." *Hats,* October 1951, p. 3.
"grasping a birdcage." *Holiday,* March 1953, p. 30.
"I want mannequins . . ." *Vogue,* February 1954, p. 84.
83 "men are going . . ." *Harper's Bazaar,* April 1957, p. 14.
88 "Notwithstanding the continued practice . . ." *Hats,* February 1957, p. 1.
89 "Just because the other women . . ." *Hats,* March 1955, p. 1,
"comb out their bobby pins . . ." *Hats,* August 1950, p. 7.
"A hat makes me look . . ." quoted in *Hats,* February 1956, p. 16.
90 "Women look as if . . ." *The New York Times,* January 1, 1958, p. 36.
"What could be more flattering . . ." *Hats,* June 1959, p. 9.
"Who doesn't wear a hat . . ." *Vogue,* October 15, 1959, p. 67.
"Excuse me . . ." *Hats,* May 1958, p. 1.

THE 60s

93 "The mood of Paris . . ." *Women's Wear Daily,* August 4, 1965, p. 1.
"jeune fille . . ." *Vogue,* July 1966, p. 100.
94 "weighs more with her makeup on . . ." quoted in *Esquire,* July 1961, p. 77.
"What has size . . ." *Vogue,* October 1, 1963, p. 140.
"A well-groomed 12-year-old . . ." *Life,* July 16, 1965, p. 88.
money spent on clothing . . . *Fortune,* October 1967, p. 162.
97 "There is Sonny . . ." *Women's Wear Daily,* August 19, 1965, p. 4.
99 "like a little Vermont . . ." *Vogue,* September 1, 1960, p. 223.
"between an egg . . ." *Hats,* August 1960, p. 6.
100 "a huge black silk cabbage . . ." *Vogue,* April 15, 1960, p. 45.
101 "One of our national . . ." *Ladies' Home Journal,* July 1962, p. 56.
102 "For the smart woman . . ." *Vogue,* September 1, 1962, p. 157.
"a rush of trippers . . ." *Vogue,* September 1, 1963, p. 165.
103 "eyebrows blotted out . . ." *Harper's Bazaar,* February, 1963, p. 122.
105 "Try a thousand . . ." *Vogue,* January 1, 1965, p. 105.
108 "almost an affront . . ." quoted in David Bailey and Peter Evans, *Goodbye Baby and Amen: A Saraband for the Sixties* (New York: Coward-McCann, 1969), p. 172.
"one thousand per cent . . ." *Vogue,* November 1, 1966, p. 194.
109 "A hard line . . ." *Vogue,* September 15, 1967, p. 85.
110 "even though it isn't easy . . ." *Hats,* February 1967, p. 19.
"string it out . . ." *Vogue,* July 1, 1969, p. 67.
112 "snips and scraps . . ." *Vogue,* July 1969, p. 68.

HAT LORE

114 "I am afraid . . ." *Daily News,* June 8, 1990, p. 54.
"Making hats is tremendously . . ." *Esquire,* August 1975, pp. 138, 72.

"shriek over a mistake . . . *The New Yorker,* April 4, 1942, p. 20.
"I would talk . . ." *The New York Times,* January 2, 1990, p. 5.
115 "the Daché millinery madhouse . . ." *The New Yorker,* October 16, 1937, p. 65.
"What I pinch . . ." *Saturday Evening Post,* February 17, 1962, p. 26.
"If a hat doesn't . . ." *Saturday Evening Post,* February 17, 1962, p. 25.
"Criticizing a hat . . ." *Time,* March 30, 1959, p. 82.

Photo Credits

The author gratefully acknowledges the photographers, publications, galleries, museums, and individuals who have provided photographs and illustrations for this book.

Portraits by John Dugdale: 2 (Model: Jill Peters); 5 (Model: Page Starzinger. Brooch courtesy Mark Walsh Collecting, Yonkers, New York); 14 (Model: Clare Hagan); 22 (Model: Gay Bryant. Hat courtesy Dorothy Weaver/Source III, New York); 26 (Model: Rebecca Wright. Hat courtesy Dorothy Weaver/Source III, New York); 29 (Model: Jane Marshall); 30 (Model: Masha Calloway); 33 (Model: Honey Twigg); 36 (Model: Margarita Mayoral); 39 (Model: Kara Sullivan. Hat courtesy of Dorothy Weaver/Source III, New York); 42 (Model: Page Starzinger. Earrings courtesy Mark Walsh Collecting, Yonkers, New York); 45 (Model: Linda Mason. Hat courtesy Dorothy Weaver/Source III, New York); 46 (Model: Ana Roth); 48 (Model: Marian Ferrara. Hat courtesy Dorothy Weaver/Source III, New York); 51 (Model: Muriel Favaro); 52 (Model: Pouran); 57 (Model: Marilyn Cooperman); 58 (Model: Liz Samolyk); 66/67 (Models: left, Ellen Carey, right, Angel Dormer); 69 (Model: Sheleigh Knollinger); 71 (Model: Sheleigh Knollinger); 72 (Model: Maria Joseph); 76 (Model: Priscilla Flood); 80 (Model: Sheila Parkert); 85 (Model: Nancy Manter. Hat courtesy Harriet Greenfield); 87 (Model: Miriam Dalton. Hat courtesy Harriet Greenfield); 91 (Model: Azy Schecter); 92 (Model: Clare Hagan); 96 (Model: Page Starzinger); 103 (Model: Elizabeth Grubaugh); 106 (Model: Carla Grande).

Additional photographs by Paul Lachenauer, courtesy The Metropolitan Museum of Art, New York: 16 (gift of Mrs. Andrew E. Beer); 18 above; 19 above (gift of Janet Jackson Wilson). Below (gift of Carl R. Bottomley, Jr.); 21 above and below; 24 left and right; 27 (gift in memory of Elizabeth Lawrence); 40 left and right (gift of Virginia Pope); 44 (gift of Eleanor Montgomery); 59 left (gift of Charles Hollerith). Right (gift of Kay Sullivan Cooney); 62 above (gift of Sally Victor). Below (gift of Charles Hollerith); 78 (gift of Shirley S. Katzenbach); 79 (gift of Charlotte R. Gutman); 84 right; 86 below (gift of James H. M. Partington); 89 left (gift of Claudia de Osborne); 94 below; 99 above; 101 above (gift of Joanne Tour Cummings). Below (gift of Glady Whitfield Solomon); 102 below (gift of Janet Sloane); 104 below left (gift of Mrs. Mortimer Solomon). Below right (gift of Glady Whitfield Solomon); 107 above (gift of The Fashion Group); 109 below left (gift of Doris Duke). Below right (gift of Mrs. Joseph B. Ziegler); 110 above (gift of *Emme*); 112; **courtesy Jody Shields collection:** endpapers; 35; 74; 75 above; 90.

Courtesy Edward C. Blum Design Lab, Fashion Institute of Technology, New York: 6; 25 below; 49 above; 56 above; 64; 81 above and below; 82; 83 below; 86 above; 88; 98; 100 left; 105

Courtesy *Vogue.* Copyright © by The Conde Nast Publications, Inc: 12 Copyright © 1945 (renewed 1973), photo: Erwin Blumenfeld; 13 Copyright © 1963 (renewed 1991), photo: David Bailey; 32 Copyright © 1931 (renewed 1959 and 1987), photo: Delnau; 47 Copyright © 1937 (renewed 1965), photo: Horst; 54 Copyright © 1945 (renewed 1973), photo: John Rawlings; 55 Center: Copyright © 1942 (renewed 1970), photo: Toni Frissell; 63 Copyright © 1944 (renewed 1972), photo: John Rawlings; 70 Copyright © 1947 (renewed 1975) 77 Copyright © 1951 (renewed 1979), photo: Erwin Blumenfeld; 95 Copyright © 1969, photo: Patrick Lichfield; 108 Copyright © 1965, photo: Bert Stern; 110 Copyright © 1969, photo: John Cowan; 111 Copyright © 1969, photo: Jack Robinson

Other sources: 3 Courtesy Don Marshall; 8 Jarmila Novotna, Courtesy Don Marshall; 10 *The New York Times;* 28 below: Washburn Gallery, New York, photo: James Abbe; 34 Courtesy Don Marshall; 41 above: Copyright © J. H. Lartigue/Photo Researchers; 49 below: UPI/Bettmann; 50 UPI/Bettmann; 56 below: Leonard McCanbe, *Life* © 1947 Time Warner, Inc.; 65 Courtesy Don Marshall; 68 Courtesy Culver Pictures; 75 below: UPI/Bettmann; 84 left: Courtesy L'Official de la Couture; 100 right: Courtesy Don Marshall; 102 above: Courtesy AP/Wide World Photos; 104 above: Courtesy AP/Wide World Photos; 107 below: Courtesy AP/Wide World Photos; 109 above: Terence Spencer, *Life* © Time Warner, Inc.

selected bibliography

Aswell, Mary. **The World of Carmel Snow.** New York: McGraw-Hill, 1962.

Bailey, David, and Peter Evans. **Goodbye Baby and Amen: A Saraband for the Sixties.** New York: Coward-McCann, 1969.

Ballard, Bettina. **In My Fashion.** New York: David McKay, 1960.

Battersby, Michael. **The Decorative Thirties.** New York: Walker & Co., 1971.

———. **The Decorative Twenties.** New York: Walker & Co., 1969.

Beaton, Cecil. **Book of Beauty.** London: Duckworth, 1930.

———. **Cecil Beaton's New York.** New York: J. B. Lippincott, 1938.

———. **Cecil Beaton's Scrapbook.** London: B. T. Batsford, 1937.

———. **The Glass of Fashion.** New York: J. B. Lippincott, 1938.

Bender, Marylin. **The Beautiful People.** New York: Coward-McCann, 1967.

Bradley, Carolyn G. **Western World Costume.** New York: Appleton-Century-Crofts, 1954.

Burris-Meyer, Elizabeth. **This Is Fashion.** New York: Harper, 1943.

Charles-Roux, Edmonde. **Chanel: Her Life, Her World, and the Woman Behind the Legend She Created.** New York: Alfred A. Knopf, 1975.

Cierplikowski, A. N. **Antoine.** New York: Prentice-Hall, 1945.

Coleman, Elizabeth Ann. **Changing Fashions, 1800–1970.** The Brooklyn Museum, 1972.

Daché, Lily. **Talking Through My Hats.** New York: Coward-McCann, 1946.

de Pougy, Liane. **My Blue Notebooks.** New York: Harper & Row, 1980.

Dior, Christian. **Dior by Dior.** London: Weidenfeld & Nicolson, 1957.

Fairchild, John. **The Fashionable Savages.** Garden City, N.Y.: Doubleday, 1965.

Flanner, Janet. **Paris Was Yesterday, 1925–1939.** New York: Viking, 1972.

Gallico, Paul. **The Revealing Eye: Personalities of the Twenties.** New York: Atheneum, 1967.

Hommage à Schiaparelli. Paris: Musée de la Mode et du Costume, 1984.

Howell, Georgina. **In Vogue.** New York: Schocken Books, 1976.

Keenan, Brigid. **The Women We Wanted to Look Like.** New York: St. Martin's, 1972.

Lanoux, Armand. **Paris in the Twenties.** New York: Golden Griffin Books, 1960.

Lynam, Ruth. **Couture.** New York: Doubleday, 1972.

Milbank Carolyn Rennolds. **Couture: The Great Designers.** New York: Stewart, Tabori, & Chang, 1985.

———. **New York Fashion.** New York: Harry N. Abrams, 1989.

Mulvagh, Jane. **Vogue History of Twentieth Century Fashion.** New York: Viking, 1988.

Nadelhoffer, Hans. **Cartier: Jewelers Extraordinary.** New York: Harry N. Abrams, 1984.

Nichols, Beverly. **The Sweet and Twenties.** London: Weidenfeld & Nicolson, 1958.

Probert, Christina. **Hats in Vogue.** New York: Abbeville, 1981.

Quant, Mary. **Quant by Quant.** New York: G. D. Putnam's Sons, 1966.

Schiaparelli, Elsa. **Shocking Life.** New York: E. P. Dutton, 1954.

Steele, Valery. **Fashion and Eroticism: Ideals of Feminine Beauty from the Victorian Era to the Jazz Age.** New York: Oxford University Press, 1985.

———. **Paris Fashion: A Cultural History.** New York: Oxford University Press, 1988.

Trahey, Jane, ed. **Harper's Bazaar: 100 Years of the American Female.** New York: Random House, 1967.

Veronese, Giulia. **Style and Design.** New York: George Brazilier, 1968.

Vreeland, Diana. **DV.** New York: Alfred A. Knopf, 1984.

White, Palmer. **Elsa Schiaparelli, Empress of Paris Fashion.** New York: Rizzoli, 1986.

———. **Poiret.** New York: Clarkson Potter, 1973.

Wiser, William. **The Crazy Years: Paris in the Twenties.** New York: Atheneum, 1983.

Yves Saint-Laurent. New York: Costume Institute, Metropolitan Museum of Art, 1983.

PERIODICALS

American Milliner

L'Art et la Mode

Art et Style

California Stylist

Chapeau de Paris

Chapeau Moderne

The Cleveland Plain Dealer

Collier's

Contemporary Modes

The Daily News (New York)

The Delineator

Dry Goods Economist

Esquire

Fashion

Fashionable Dress

Fashion Accessories

Fashion Arts

Fashion Digest

Fashion's Art

Femina

La Femme Chic

Flair

Fortune

Harper's Bazaar

Hats

Holiday

Illustrated Milliner

Junior League Bulletin

Kaleidoscope

The Ladies' Home Journal

Life

Look

Mademoiselle

Millinery and Accessories

Millinery Digest

Millinery Monitor

Millinery Trade Review

The New Yorker

The New York Times

L'Officiel

Pictorial Review

The Saturday Evening Post

Style Arts

Time

Vogue

Women's Wear Daily

Lacknowledgments**J**

I am indebted to a number of people who were generous with their help, fair-minded with their sympathy, and stoic with their patience, notably Allison Kyle Leopold, Ann Shakeshaft, Linda Mason, and Catherine Laroche.

I am infinitely obliged to my editor, Lauren Shakely, for her unflagging humor and expertise.

Thank you to John Dugdale for his singular vision and his shabby good-luck equipment. Thank you too to Honey Twigg for her wonderful artistry and to Paul Lachenauer for his inspired work on the still-life photography.

Helene Silverman deserves a special acknowledgment for her design of this book. Appreciation also goes to her assistant, Frank Gargiulo.

For their help at various stages, I'd like to thank: Eugenia Bartels, Lizi Boyd, Shelley Boyd, Charles Bumgardner, Nigel Carr, Christine Wang Chang, Pam Choy, Martin Cooke, Corinna, Isabella Ginanneschi, Carla Grande, Joan Gustafson, Harriet Love, Tamara and Leon Schneider, Edna and Leo Shields, Debra Turner, Abraham Voyster, Dorothy Weaver, Jane and Fuschia Wildgoose, and Carl Wolf. From the Costume Insitute of the Metropolitan Museum of Art in New York, my appreciation to Katell le Boorhis and Kim Fink, and Harold Koda and Don Patrillo of New York's Fashion Institute of Technology. Diana Edkins of Conde Nast and Don Marshall were generous with photographs and information. Special appreciation is due to my agent, Deborah Geltman.

To the many people at Clarkson Potter who helped produce *Hats,* I am particularly grateful: Joan Denman, Laura Starrett, Catherine Sustana, and Jane Treuhaft.

[index]